Amazing Appellations

Dennis + Luanne Lovin

Amazing Appellations

—∽—

DISCOVERING THE NAMES OF JESUS

Kristina Howard-Booth

Sojourner's Journey

For Matt and Jordan,
your support means more than you will ever know.

Contents

"JESUS! The name that refreshes the fainting spirits of humbled sinners; sweet to speak and sweet to hear,
Jesus, a Savior!"

Matthew Henry

Appellation

An appellation is an identifying name or title that reveals an aspect of character. There are more than one hundred fifty appellations ascribed to Jesus in the Bible; each one affirms a unique characteristic belonging to Him. By learning the names of Jesus, the treasure of redemption and relationship will be discovered. The Amazing Appellations declare the steadfast love and faithfulness of the Lord for all people.

1

∽

Gospel Introductions

All relationships begin with an introduction; it is how we have our first interaction with someone. The Oxford English Dictionary defines an introduction as "a formal presentation of one person to another, in which each is told the other's name." The New Testament begins with each of the Gospel writers, Matthew, Mark, Luke, and John, introducing us to Jesus by giving us His names. He already knows our names, thus, making the introduction complete. Each name used to introduce us to Jesus is unique to Him and reveals His purpose on earth.

Jesus

"She will bear a son, and you shall call his name Jesus, for he will save his people from their sins."
Matthew 1:21

The hope and salvation of the world are found in the name of Jesus, "for He will save His people from their sins." In Hebrew, Jesus means "Jehovah the Savior" or "Jehovah is Salvation;" no other name has that kind of power and eternal significance. The angel Gabriel explained this to Mary, "And behold, you will conceive in your womb and bear a son, and you shall call his name Jesus. He will be great and will be called the Son of the Most High. And the Lord God will give to him the throne of his father David, and he will reign over the house of Jacob forever, and of his kingdom, there will be no end." (Luke 1:31-33) Salvation was coming; all the promises the Lord had made to His people were going to be fulfilled by the child Mary was going to have, and His name was to announce it all, Jesus.

PRAYER:

Lord Jesus, we praise Your name. There is no other name that brings hope and salvation to the world. Thank You for being our salvation, for loving us enough to come and pay the debt of sin we could never pay. Through Your life, death, and resurrection, You conquered sin, death, and hell for all time, securing eternal salvation for all who follow You. Thank You for being the name above every other name, Jesus. May we give You all the praise and glory and honor. Amen

Immanuel

> *"All this took place to fulfill what the Lord had spoken by the prophet: 'Behold, the virgin shall conceive and bear a son,*
> *and they shall call his name Immanuel'*
> *(which means, God with us)."*
> Matthew 1:22-23

The name Immanuel or Emmanuel, depending on which Bible translation you are using, is a combination of two words; "El," God, and "emmanu," with us; to unmistakably mean "God with us." In the Hebrew Bible, Yahweh, the Lord, tells His people, "I am with you" one hundred fourteen times. With the arrival of Jesus, which can be translated as Yahweh saves, the Lord declares, after four hundred years of silence, "I am with you. My divine presence is physically among you." Reminding the people that He had never left them, He faithfully fulfilled the promise He made to king Ahaz through the prophet Isaiah seven hundred years before. "And he said, "Hear then, O house of David! Is it too little for you to weary men, that you weary my God also? Therefore the Lord himself will give you a sign. Behold, the virgin shall conceive and bear a son, and shall call his name Immanuel." (Isaiah 7:13-14)

God is still with us, even though we may feel that we are experiencing long periods of silence like the Israelites. Remember, the Lord never left them. He was at work getting everything ready for His perfect timing to reveal the best opportunity for your life to have maximum impact. I know waiting is difficult, but have faith and trust Immanuel.

Prayer:

Lord, Immanuel, it is an overwhelming comfort to know that you are with us, always. When we feel alone, we can trust that You are there. When we think all is silence, we can trust that You are still by our side, working things out for our good. Thank You for always being with us. Amen

Son of God

"The beginning of the gospel of Jesus Christ, the Son of God."
Mark 1:1

Mark wastes no time identifying who Jesus is and what He has done, emphasizing the importance of his gospel; it is the good news that changes everything. "The Son of God title was used here to attract attention and secure the respect of those who should read the gospel. It is no common history. It does not recount the deals of a man – of a hero or a philosopher – but the doctrines and doings of the Son of God." (Barnes) For the Jewish people of the time, this title denoted equality with God and was the main characteristic of the Messiah they had been awaiting. Mark quickly backs up his declaration by quoting Malachi and Isaiah and giving a brief account of John the Baptist. John was "the voice of the one crying in the wilderness, "prepare the way of the Lord, make his paths straight" (Mark 1:3) before jumping into the ministry of Jesus.

The foundation of the Gospel, of salvation, of all we believe as Christ-followers is wrapped up in this verse; "The beginning of the gospel of Jesus Christ, the Son of God." Do you recognize that Jesus Christ is the very Son of God? The answer does indeed change everything. Do you need to wrestle with the work Jesus has done? Jesus, the Son of God, has come "proclaiming the gospel of God,and saying, 'The time is fulfilled, and the kingdom of God is at hand; repent and believe in the gospel.'" (Mark 1:14-15)

Prayer:

Jesus, thank You for coming to earth, giving up all Your heavenly comfort, yet, staying God while becoming man to save us. You are the One we all search for; You are the Messiah, the Son of God. Amen

Son of the Most High

"He will be great and will be called the Son of the Most High. And the Lord God will give to him the throne of his father David, and he will reign over the house of Jacob forever, and of his kingdom there will be no end."
Luke 1:32-33

God Most High is the name by which Melchizedek, king, and priest of Salem, referred to the Lord as he blessed Abram; "And he blessed him and said, "Blessed be Abram by God Most High, Possessor of heaven and earth; and blessed be God Most High, who has delivered your enemies into your hand!" And Abram gave him a tenth of everything." (Genesis 14:19-20) The title speaks of God's "absolute perfection in Himself, and His sovereign dominion over all the creatures." (Benson)

Jesus Christ, Son of the Most High, is the fulfillment of God Most High's promise to the people of Israel; "then a throne will be established in steadfast love, and on it will sit in faithfulness in the tent of David one who judges and seeks justice and is swift to do righteousness." (Isaiah 16:5) The Lord, God Most High, was pronouncing Jesus, hundreds of years before He was born, to be His Son and King over all things. This title has always been assigned to Jesus; the demons acknowledge and cower at His power, as demonstrated by the demon that possessed the man at Gerasenes; "And crying out with a loud voice, he said, "What have you to do with me, Jesus, Son of the Most High God? I adjure you by God, do not torment me." (Mark 5:7) Jesus is great, and His kingdom has no end. He is with God and is God (John 1:1). He is the Son of the Most High.

Prayer:

Jesus, You are Son of the Most High; even the demons know it. Thank You for being the fulfillment of God's promises and for bringing salvation to all who believe in You. Thank You for being the one who "seeks justice and is swift to do righteousness." Thank You that Your kingdom is forever and is "established in steadfast love." Amen

The Word

"In the beginning was the Word, and the Word was with God, and the Word was God. He was in the beginning with God."
John 1:1-2

One of the most significant aspects of Jesus revealed in the New Testament is that Jesus is the Word. John goes back to the eternity before creation to show that Jesus has always existed; He is divine and eternal. The Word is not someone or something other than God; He is God and is intrinsic to God's unique identity. Throughout the Old Testament and Jewish Scriptures, the Word is the personified knowledge of God imparted through the prophets and the law for the people to follow to accomplish God's will. Jesus fulfills all the Old Testament ideals; He is God in human form, personally communicating the will of God, His love, and his desire to reconcile us to Him by becoming flesh and paying the price for our sins. "And the Word became flesh and dwelt among us, and we have seen his glory, glory as of the only Son from the Father, full of grace and truth." (John 1:14) "He came to his own, and his own people did not receive him.But to all who did receive him, who believed in his name, he gave the right to become children of God." (John 1:11-12)

Prayer:

Jesus, the Word, how holy and precious is your name; all creation is from You and sustained by You. Thank You for coming to be with us, for making a way for us to be with the Father and understand His love and His will for our lives. Thank You for Your grace and your truth. Amen

Christ

"For unto you is born this day in the city of David a Savior, who is Christ the Lord."
Luke 2:11

The hope and power wrapped up in the title "Christ" is immense; it is the "good news of great joy that will be for all the people." (Luke 2:10) The Christ, the Messiah, was about to be born. Christos, the Greek word from which we get Christ, is the Greek translation of the Hebrew word Messiah; it occurs over five hundred times in the Greek New Testament as the designated title for Jesus. Christ the Lord implies, "the Messiah spoken of by the prophets; the anointed of the Lord, with the Holy Ghost without measure, to be a prophet, priest, and king in his church; and who is the true Jehovah, the Lord our righteousness, the Lord of all creatures, the Lord of angels, good and bad, the Lord of all men, as Creator, the Prince of the kings of the earth, the Lord of lords, and King of kings." (Gill) Jesus is Christ; He is the promised Messiah fulfilled.

Prayer:

Christ Jesus, You are "the good news of great joy," You are the Messiah, the deliverer of all people, our salvation. Great is Your name and worthy of all our praise. May You receive all glory and honor as Christ the Lord! Amen

Sunrise

> *"because of the tender mercy of our God,*
> *whereby the sunrise shall visit us from on high*
> *to give light to those who sit in darkness and in*
> *the shadow of death, to guide our feet into the*
> *way of peace."*
> *Luke 1:78-79*

How beautifully does the Sunrise express "the tender mercy of our God upon us"? Jesus is the Rising Sun (NIV), the Dayspring (KJV), which gently brightens the sky of our life before bursting over the horizon in magnificent radiance, instantly dissolving the darkness of sin and death when we accept Jesus as our Savior. As humans, we deal with darkness in many forms; but as Christ-followers, "you who fear my name (the Lord), the sun of righteousness (Jesus) shall rise with healing in its wings." (Malachi 4:2 emphasis mine) Only Jesus can fully heal all the wounds of darkness and death "to guide our feet into the way to peace." Once we have the Sunrise, we cannot be entirely overtaken by darkness again. Jesus promised, "I have come into the world as light, so that believers in me may not remain in darkness." (John 12:46) Let each sunrise remind you of the tender mercy and healing of the Lord.

Prayer:

Thank You, Lord Jesus, for being the Sunrise, for breaking through the darkness of this world to bring us light, healing, mercy, and peace. As the Sun, You are always there, bringing life, and darkness cannot overtake You. You give us new days and new mercies. May we be reminded of You by every sunrise we see. Amen

Horn of Salvation

"and has raised up a horn of salvation for us
in the house of his servant David,"
Luke 1:69

In Biblical times the horn symbolized strength and might. The Lord brought about His mighty plan of salvation through Jesus Christ, whose life, death, and resurrection conquered sin and death for all eternity. The Lord fulfilled His promise to David; "And David spoke to the Lord the words of this song on the day when the Lord delivered him from the hand of all his enemies, and from the hand of Saul. He said, 'The Lord is my rock and my fortress and my deliverer, my God, my rock, in whom I take refuge, my shield, and the horn of my salvation, my stronghold and my refuge, my savior; you save me from violence.'" (2 Samuel 22:1-3) Zechariah, a priest and father of John the Baptist, sang about the Lord fulfilling the promise; Jesus Christ, the Horn of Salvation, was about to be born. We should all rejoice as Zechariah did; the Horn of Salvation has risen.

Prayer:

Lord Jesus, Horn of Salvation, You conquered sin, death, and hell to bring eternal life to those who accept You. You are my Savior in whom I take refuge. May I rejoice and sing of Your strength and might all my days. Amen

Savior

> *"And the angel said to them, "Fear not, for behold, I bring you good news of great joy that will be for all the people. For unto you is born this day in the city of David a Savior,"*
> *Luke 2:10-11a*

Savior is a distinctive title, instantly generating images of God saving and delivering His people. The Gospel, according to Luke, focuses on the grace, mercy, power, and authority of Jesus as Savior. Mary and Zechariah acknowledge their need for a savior before Jesus' birth and praised the Lord for what He was going to do through Him: "Blessed be the Lord God of Israel, for he has visited and redeemed his people and has raised up a horn of salvation for us in the house of his servant David... And you, child, will be called the prophet of the Most High; for you will go before the Lord to prepare his ways, to give knowledge of salvation to his people in the forgiveness of their sins, because of the tender mercy of our God." (Luke 1:68-78a) Simeon and Anna acknowledge Jesus as Savior when He is brought to the temple as a baby exclaiming, "Lord, now you are letting your servant depart in peace, according to your word; for my eyes have seen your salvation that you have prepared in the presence of all peoples... And coming up at that very hour, she began to give thanks to God and to speak of him to all who were waiting for the redemption of Jerusalem." (Luke 2:29-38) The Savior they had been waiting for had arrived. He is our Savior also, "his name is called Jesus, because He saves from sin, from Satan, from the law, from the world, from death, and hell, and wrath to come and from every enemy." (Gill) Celebrate the Good News; "And Jesus said to him, "Today salvation has come to this house, since he also is a son of Abraham. For the Son of Man came to seek and to save the lost." (Luke 19:9-10)

Prayer:

Savior, we worship You and praise You for all You have done for us. You have saved us from sin, death, and hell. You have covered us in Your righteousness. Thank You for Your mercy, grace, and love. Amen

Consolation of Israel

"Now there was a man in Jerusalem, whose name was Simeon, and this man was righteous and devout, waiting for the consolation of Israel, and the Holy Spirit was upon him."
Luke 2:25

The Consolation of Israel is a beautiful, common phrase used in Jewish prayer to refer to the Messiah for whom they were waiting. The idea of everlasting comfort and counsel from the Lord's Christ is encompassed in this title. Consolation refers to a person's comfort when going through difficult and disappointing times. Israel was waiting for the one who could bring them out of all their hardship, as are we. Yet, the Consolation has come; Jesus Christ is our comforter and counselor. He has saved us from sin, death, and hell. We can rest in Him, no matter the difficulties we are facing. He is the Messiah, the Consolation of Israel. Are you resting in the Consolation of Jesus Christ?

Prayer:

Lord Jesus, You are the Consolation of Israel; the wait is over. You are my comforter and counselor. You give me comfort during times of trouble and hardship, and that comfort will never end; You are always with me. You have saved me from sin and death, giving me eternal life, the ultimate consolation. To You go all glory and honor. Amen

Creator

> *"All things were made through him, and without him was not any thing made that was made."*
>
> *John 1:3*

Jesus is God (John 1:1), Creator of all things. We read the creation account in Genesis 1 or the Lord's description of His mighty work in Job 38, and we barely scratch the surface of what being Creator means. It can be difficult for us to wrap our brains around this fact, which is why Scripture tells us, "He was in the world, and the world was made through him, yet the world did not know him. He came to his own, and his own people did not receive him. But to all who did receive him, who believed in his name, he gave the right to become children of God." (John 1:10-12) We do not have to understand it all; we have faith to accept it. Jesus is the Creator of all things, and as your Creator, He loves you. In fact, He loves you so much that He came here, lived a sinless life, was crucified to pay the debt of your sins, and rose again, defeating sin, death, and hell for all time. Jesus did that for you. He created you and loves you; He has proven it.

Prayer:

Creator, everything is made by You, from the most microscopic particle to the grandest galaxy. You created and control it all. Although you created us, we struggle to understand what that means sometimes, but You love us enough to be patient; so that we can know You. Thank You for the promise that when we receive You, we secure the right to become children of God. Thank You for being our loving Creator.

Life

"In him was life, and the life was the light of men."
John 1:4

Jesus is life, by every definition we have of the word and beyond. Jesus is the Creator of life and has all authority over it, "He was in the beginning with God. All things were made through him, and without him was not any thing made that was made. In him was life, and the life was the light of men." (John 1:2-4) Jesus came to give us abundant life, "The thief comes only to steal and kill and destroy. I came that they may have life and have it abundantly." (John 10:10) Jesus gave up His life so that we could have eternal life. "And this is the testimony, that God gave us eternal life, and this life is in his Son. Whoever has the Son has life; whoever does not have the Son of God does not have life. And we know that the Son of God has come and has given us understanding, so that we may know him who is true; and we are in him who is true, in His Son Jesus Christ. He is the true God and eternal life." (1 John 5:11-12, 20) Jesus, who is Life, promises us that our eternal life is secure through Him: "I give them eternal life, and they will never perish, and no one will snatch them out of my hand."

(John 10:28) He is the only one who can truthfully say, "Jesus said to him, "I am the way, and the truth, and the life. No one comes to the Father except through me." (John 14:6)

Prayer:

Jesus, You are Life, Creator, only through You is there life. Without You, there is no life. You bring us abundant life and eternal life. You guard my life against the enemy, and no one can snatch me out of Your hands; my life is secure in You. Thank You for giving us life.

Lamb of God

"The next day, he saw Jesus coming toward him and said, 'Behold, the Lamb of God, who takes away the sin of the world!'"
John 1:29

It was through the blood of a sacrificed lamb painted on the doorpost of a person's home, as the Lord instructed, that caused the Lord to Passover that home during the last plague of Egypt, the killing of the firstborn. "It is the Lord's Passover. For I will pass through the land of Egypt that night, and I will strike all the firstborn in the land of Egypt, both man and beast; and on all the gods of Egypt I will execute judgments: I am the Lord. The blood shall be a sign for you, on the houses where you are. And when I see the blood, I will pass over you, and no plague will befall you to destroy you when I strike the land of Egypt." (Exodus 12:11-13) The Jewish people commemorate Passover annually to honor what the Lord did for them.

Jesus took upon Himself all the rich symbolism of the Jewish sacrificial lamb. He was the perfect unblemished lamb sent by God as a sacrifice. His bloodshed on the cross provides atonement for our sins, covering us; so that the wrath of the Lord will Passover all who have accepted Jesus as Savior during the final judgment. "They have washed their robes and made them white in the blood of the Lamb. Therefore they are before the throne of God and serve him day and night in his temple, and he who sits on the throne will shelter them with his presence. They shall hunger no more, neither thirst any more; the sun shall not strike them, nor any scorching heat. For the Lamb in the midst of the throne will be their shepherd, and he will guide them to springs of living water, and God will wipe away every tear from their eyes." (Revelation 7:14-17)

Prayer:

Thank You, Lord, for providing the perfect Lamb of God, Jesus. It is only through the sacrifice of the Lamb of God that Your wrath will pass over me during judgment. Thank You, Jesus, for loving me enough to be that perfect Lamb. I rejoice and praise You knowing that I am washed white by Your blood and that You are my guide to living water. Amen

Redemption of Jerusalem

"And coming up at that very hour, she began to give thanks to God and to speak of him to all who were waiting for the redemption of Jerusalem."
Luke 2:38

The people of Israel were awaiting redemption, and they expected the promised Messiah, but many missed His arrival. Anna, who spent her life in prayer with complete faith that the Messiah would come, immediately knew that Jesus was the Redemption of Jerusalem. She began to praise God and tell everyone about Jesus. Have you missed Jesus? Jesus did not come to redeem just Jerusalem but all people (Luke 2:10). He did indeed redeem us. He paid the price for our sins, a debt we could never repay, through His sinless life and brutal death on the cross. His shed blood atoned for our sins. His resurrection resulted in the eternal defeat of sin, death, and hell; all who accept it can find salvation. Be like Anna, give thanks to God, and speak of Him to all who are waiting for redemption.

Prayer:

Lord Jesus, thank You for being the Redemption of Jerusalem and the Redemption of all people. Thank you for paying my sin debt and redeeming my life; it is a debt I could not repay; now, I have eternal life. Lord, let me speak with boldness of Your redemption to all who seek You.

King of the Jews

"Where is he who has been born king of the Jews? For we saw his star when it rose and have come to worship him."
Matthew 2:2

"Where is he who has been born king of the Jews? For we saw his star when it rose and have come to worship him;" these words were spoken to the Jews, or rather to Herod, the king of Jewish people at that time, causing great confusion among the political and religious leaders. The wise men from the east asking for the King of the Jews "make no scruple of his being born, of this they were fully assured; nor did they in the least hesitate about his being king of the Jews who was born, but only inquire where he was." (Gill) Prophecies from Isaiah and Daniel had everyone, not just the Jews, awaiting the great king that was to arise from the Jewish people and triumph over tyranny; expectations were high.

Jesus, however, came into the world not as a triumphal king but as a baby, born of a poor, ordinary family; thus, most of the world missed his arrival. The King of the Jews had come and would later die with that very title nailed above his head as the crime for which He was crucified; three days later, He would rise, having defeated sin and death, proving to be not only the King of the Jews but "Lord of lords and King of kings!" (Revelation 17:14)

Prayer:

Jesus, You are King, King of the Jews, and King of kings! Your kingdom will reign forever. Thank You for coming as promised. I am sorry your arrival is so often missed, even by those who should know what to look for. Lord, help me see You for who You are and all You have done for me. Thank You, my King.

Messiah

*"He first found his own brother Simon and
said to him, "We have found the Messiah"
(which means Christ)."*
John 1:41

Messiah, the One the Jewish nation had been waiting for,
had come, and Andrew was eager to tell his brother he had
found Him. The title Messiah speaks to the expectation of the
anointed king that God would send to restore His people. The
Messiah would be their Savior and Redeemer, the Deliverer
of Israel long ago promised. Jesus Christ is the Messiah; He
fulfilled God's promises and purposes for His people in every
way. "Now Jesus did many other signs in the presence of the
disciples, which are not written in this book;but these are
written so that you may believe that Jesus is the Christ, the Son
of God, and that by believing you may have life in his name."
(John 20:30-31) Through Jesus, we have hope. His life, death,
and resurrection defeated sin and restored our relationship
with the Lord, giving us the promise of eternal life with Him.
Jesus is the Messiah.

Prayer:

Jesus, Messiah, You are the Anointed King. Your kingdom will reign forever. Thank You for delivering me from sin and restoring my relationship with the Lord. Thank You for fulfilling all of God's promises. Let me be as excited as Andrew to tell all I meet I have found the Messiah.

2

Prophesied Titles

Prophecy is the foretelling of what is to come. Throughout the Old Testament, names and titles foreshadow the coming Messiah, the One who would deliver the people of Israel and make them the great nation the Lord had promised. All of Scripture points to the faithfulness of the Lord and His plan of salvation through Jesus Christ. Each prophesied title in the Old Testament proves this as Jesus fulfills each one. Every name brings hope; every name proves the Lord keeps His promises.

Wonderful Counselor, Mighty God, Everlasting Father, Price of Peace

"For to us a child is born, to us a son is given;
and the government shall be upon his shoulder,
and his name shall be called
Wonderful Counselor, Mighty God,
Everlasting Father, Prince of Peace."
Isaiah 9:6

In this one verse, you can find four of the most compelling, descriptive names of Jesus. The prophet Isaiah described the Messiah and His kingdom that was to come, a kingdom for which the Israelites (and ultimately all people) were longing. It was common during Isaiah's time for kings to have titles broadcasting their accomplishments to the people. Jesus, the prophesied king, is no different; each title is rooted in His kingship. Therefore, each name depicts a characteristic that could only belong to the Lord Jesus Christ.

Wonderful Counselor references the king's role as the nation's political guide and denotes the personal counsel --

guidance, teaching, comfort – to be given. John Calvin explains, "the Redeemer will come endowed with absolute wisdom...it is not, therefore, because he knows all his father's secrets that the prophet calls him Counselor, but, rather because, preceding from the bosom of the Father, he is in every respect the highest and perfect teacher." (Calvin) Jesus is wisdom incarnate; He did not run and hide from evil but confronted and conquered it forever on the cross with perfect wisdom. There is no better counselor, no one who understands life and death better than Jesus. "When the cares of my heart are many, your consolations cheer my soul." (Psalm 94:19)

The military strength of Jesus, our Mighty God, is emphasized. Might refers to power in battle; Jesus is undefeated! He has conquered all foes, including sin, hell, and death. He is a warrior and provides us armor; He is "our strength and shield," protecting us from eternal enemies. (See Ephesians 6) Jesus is our Mighty God, and we do not have to be afraid.

Jesus is eternal. He has always been and always will be; "I am the Alpha and the Omega, the first and the last, the beginning and the end." (Revelation 22:13) Everlasting Father speaks to His eternal nature along with His love and goodness. The passion shown by Jesus as He provides for our needs is more than any earthly parent could give to a child. Jesus reminds us of this during the Sermon on the Mount; "If you then, who are evil, know how to give good gifts to your children, how much more will your Father who is in heaven give good things to those who ask him!" (Matthew 7:11)

Jesus is the Prince of Peace by virtue of His wonderful counsel, might, and love. Jesus brings peace to His people. We can attain peace by knowing that our Mighty God, Jesus, has defeated sin and death and is seated on His throne in heaven. Our Everlasting Father has restored our relationship, and one day we will join Him in His eternal kingdom. While we are here, He is our Wonderful Counselor guiding us in all the ways we should go, bringing us hope and peace.

Prayer:

Lord, thousands of years ago, You promised a Wonderful Counselor, Mighty God, Everlasting Father, Prince of Peace, and You fulfilled that promise through Jesus Christ. Jesus brings comfort and peace; He is all-powerful and infinite. Thank You for keeping Your promises. Thank You for Jesus.

Cornerstone

"Therefore thus says the Lord God, 'Behold,
I am the one who has laid as a foundation in
Zion, a stone, a tested stone, a precious corner-
stone, of a sure foundation: 'Whoever believes
will not be in haste.'"
Isaiah 28:16

Cornerstones carry the weight of a building; they stabilize and hold together the foundation; Jesus is the Cornerstone of all that the Lord is building. The eternal Kingdom of God rests on the Cornerstone of Jesus Christ. Jesus carried all the weight of our sins and took the punishment we deserve for them. He is the foundation of salvation and redemption, defeating sin, death, and hell through His life, crucifixion, and resurrection. Jesus is our Cornerstone, our secure foundation, which will not crumble or fade. Peter reminds us of this point in his letter to the exiles: "As you come to him, a living stone rejected by men but in the sight of God chosen and precious, you your-selves like living stones are being built up as a spiritual house, to be a holy priesthood, to offer spiritual sacrifices acceptable to God through Jesus Christ. For it stands in Scripture: "Behold, I am laying in Zion a stone, a cornerstone chosen and precious, and whoever believes in him will not be put to shame." So the honor is for you who believe, but for those who do not believe, "The stone that the builders rejected has become the cornerstone." (1 Peter 2:4-7) Paul also expresses this relationship in his letter to the Ephesians: "So then you are no longer strangers and aliens, but you are fellow citizens with the saints and members of the household of God, built on the foundation of the apostles and prophets, Christ Jesus himself being the cornerstone, in whom the whole structure, being joined together, grows into a holy temple in the Lord." (Ephesians 2:19-21) Building our lives around the Cornerstone, Jesus Christ, means we have nothing to fear.

Prayer:

Thank You, Jesus, for being my Cornerstone. Nothing life throws at me can cause You to crack or crumble; You carry the weight of salvation as my secure foundation. Eternal life in heaven is definite when founded on You, the chosen and precious Cornerstone. I have nothing to fear, for I will not be put to shame.

Holy One of Israel

"Fear not, you worm Jacob, you men of Israel!
I am the one who helps you, declares the Lord;
your Redeemer is the Holy One of Israel."
Isaiah 41:14

The "Holy One of Israel" is the prophet Isaiah's favorite expression for the Lord, using it twenty-five times in just the first five chapters of his book. To be holy is to be set apart, to be completely other; the Lord is so wholly other from us that we can barely begin to understand Him and often despise Him for His holiness. "Ah, sinful nation, a people laden with iniquity, offspring of evildoers, children who deal corruptly! They have forsaken the Lord, they have despised the Holy One of Israel, they are utterly estranged." (Isaiah 1:4) Isaiah's description of the nation and people of Judah sounds as if it could be describing any country in the world today, which can be discouraging. Yet, because "your Redeemer is the Holy One of Israel" there is hope. "Come now, let us reason together, says the Lord: though your sins are like scarlet, they shall be as white as snow; though they are red like crimson, they shall become like wool." (Isaiah 1:18). Jesus Christ washed away the scarlet stains of our sins with the blood He shed on the cross; through His life, death, and resurrection we are cleansed, made "white as snow." Only the Holy One of Israel has that power, only Jesus Christ.

Prayer:

Lord Jesus, You are our Redeemer, the Holy One of Israel. Thank You for loving people who despise You and being willing to come and wash away our sins. You are Holy and Righteous, and it is Your righteous blood that makes me white as snow. Thank You that You are the Holy One of Israel and that we have nothing to fear.

The Lord Who Sanctifies

"You are to speak to the people of Israel and say, 'Above all you shall keep my Sabbaths, for this is a sign between me and you throughout your generations, that you may know that I, the Lord, sanctify you."
Exodus 31:13

Sanctification is the process of becoming holy. Only the Lord is Holy; it is who He is; therefore, He cannot be around anyone or anything unholy. The Law served as a way for the people in Old Testament times that followed it to be sanctified. Unfortunately, like us, they could never keep the law perfectly, and atonement for sin required a sacrifice. The sacrificial system was a continual process as people continually sin. The blood of animals could never cover all sin completely, so the Lord sent Jesus to be the perfect and final sacrifice for sin. Through Jesus' death on the cross, His innocent, sinless life took on the sins of the world (past, present, and future), shedding His blood to cover them once and for all; we are sanctified.

"And by that will we have been sanctified through the offering of the body of Jesus Christ once for all. And every priest stands daily at his service, offering repeatedly the same sacrifices, which can never take away sins. But when Christ had offered for all time a single sacrifice for sins, he sat down at the right hand of God, waiting from that time until his enemies should be made a footstool for his feet. For by a single offering, he has perfected for all time those who are being sanctified. And the Holy Spirit also bears witness to us; for after saying, "This is the covenant that I will make with them after those days, declares the Lord: I will put my laws on their hearts, and write them on their minds," then he adds, "I will remember their sins and their lawless deeds no more." Where there is forgiveness of these, there is no longer any offering for sin. Therefore, brothers, since we have confidence to enter the holy places by the blood of Jesus, by the new and living way that he opened for us through the curtain, that is, through his flesh, and since we have a great priest over the house of God, let us draw near with a true heart in full assurance of faith, with our hearts sprinkled clean from an evil conscience, and our bodies washed with pure water. Let us hold fast the confession of our hope without wavering, for he who promised is faithful." (Hebrews 10:10-23)

Prayer:

Lord Jesus, thank You for being the One who sanctifies me; I could never do it on my own. You have gone before me and have sprinkled my heart clean; so that I can hold fast to the hope found in You, Jehovah M'Kaddesh, the Lord Who Sanctifies. Thank You for being the perfect and final sacrifice that brings sanctification to all who believe in You.

Redeemer

"For I know that my Redeemer lives,
and at the last he will stand upon the earth."
Job 19:25

Job declared he had a Redeemer; he trusted that the Lord, his Redeemer, was coming and would right all that was wrong, bringing salvation despite all he had been through. The word translated as Redeemer in the original Hebrew is Goel. Goel was the name given to the next of kin whose duty was to redeem, ransom, or avenge the family member who had fallen into debt or bondage. Job was confident that the Lord would take this duty upon Himself, being surety for him and avenging his quarrel; by the end of Job's life, the Lord had restored him, and Jesus Christ redeemed him completely.

Jesus is our Redeemer; He has pleaded our case before the Lord. He paid the ransom of our sin-debt by shedding His blood on the cross; we are presented blameless through Him. His death and resurrection set us free from the bondage of sin, death, and hell, guaranteeing our eternal salvation.

Prayer:

My Redeemer, Jesus, is alive, having conquered sin and death; He redeemed me by paying my debt to sin and giving me eternal life. I could thank You from now until I die, and it would never be sufficient to express the thankfulness and gratitude in my heart to You.

Healer

"for I am the Lord, your healer."
Exodus 15:26

The Lord declared His character to the Israelites as they were in Egypt, protecting them during the plaques, providing Passover, and setting them free; "for I am the Lord that healeth thee; both in body and soul; in body, by preserving from diseases, and by curing them when afflicted with them; and in soul by pardoning their iniquities. " (Gill) The Lord, being immutable, does the same for us; "Now I want to remind you, although you once fully knew it, that Jesus, who saved a people out of the land of Egypt, afterward destroyed those who did not believe." (Jude 5) Jesus cures us, those who have faith in Him, of our most deadly disease, sin. "He himself bore our sins in his body on the tree, that we might die to sin and live to righteousness. By his wounds you have been healed." (1 Peter 2:24) Jesus is our Healer; only through Him is disease and death conquered and healed. "Bless the Lord, O my soul, and forget not all his benefits, who forgives all your iniquity, who heals all your diseases." (Psalm 103:2-3) Because of Jesus, our Healer, we have hope and can trust that one day, "He will wipe away every tear from their eyes, and death shall be no more, neither shall there be mourning, nor crying, nor pain anymore, for the former things have passed away." (Revelation 21:4)

Prayer:

Healer, Jesus, we sing out, "Bless the Lord, O my soul," You have forgiven my iniquity and healed my deadliest disease, "Bless the Lord!" All my hope is found in You; in the future You have promised, in the steadfast love and faithfulness, my Healer, there will be no more pain or mourning. You will wipe away every tear. You heal me, body and soul.

Glory of the Lord

"And the glory of the Lord shall be revealed,
and all flesh shall see it together, for the mouth
of the Lord has spoken."
Isaiah 40:5

The Glory of the Lord is the manifestation of His presence and of His unique nature. Throughout the Old Testament, the Glory of the Lord was manifest in various forms of light or as a cloud of fire; the emphasis, however, is not on the form but on the absolute power and person of the Lord. The Lord revealed a clearer view of His wisdom, power, holiness, mercy, and grace in each instance. Jesus is the Light by which the Lord allows us to come face to face with Him; He is the visible revelation of the invisible Lord Almighty, displaying the grace and truth all people need. "And the Word became flesh and dwelt among us, and we have seen his glory, glory as of the only Son from the Father, full of grace and truth." (John 1:14) The cross and resurrection were the ultimate signs of Jesus' divine glory, "But rejoice insofar as you share Christ's sufferings, that you may also rejoice and be glad when his glory is revealed." (1 Peter 4:13) Jesus is the Glory of the Lord revealed, and there is coming a day "When the Son of Man comes in his glory, and all the angels with him, then he will sit on his glorious throne" (Matthew 25:31), and we will be there to see Him and worship Him forever.

Prayer:

The Glory of the Lord has been revealed; thank You, Jesus, for allowing us to come face to face with Your power, grace, and mercy. You gave Yourself to show us how much You love us and how much we need You. All glory in heaven and earth is Yours.

Branch

"Hear now, O Joshua the high priest, you and
your friends who sit before you, for they are men
who are a sign: behold, I will bring my servant the
Branch. For behold, on the stone that I have set
before Joshua, on a single stone with seven eyes, I
will engrave its inscription, declares the Lord of
hosts, and I will remove the iniquity of this land
in a single day."
Zechariah 3:8-9

Branch is an often-used title by the Old Testament prophets to describe the coming Messiah. Zechariah uses the title
as a proper name knowing all those listening would instantly
connect the Branch with Isaiah and Jeremiah's descriptive
prophecies: "There shall come forth a shoot from the stump
of Jesse, and a branch from his roots shall bear fruit." (Isaiah
11:1) "In those days and at that time I will cause a righteous
Branch to spring up for David, and he shall execute justice
and righteousness in the land." (Jeremiah 33:15) Every reference to the Branch speaks of hope rising from the remnant of
the royal line of David, coming from a lowly background to
bring righteousness and salvation. In this instance, Zechariah is

stating that "from the depressed house of David a scion should spring in whom all that was prophesied concerning the priesthood and kingdom of Israel should find its accomplishment." (Exell and Spence-Jones) Jesus, the Branch, became our High Priest fulfilling the high priest's duties once and for all; "For it was indeed fitting that we should have such a high priest, holy, innocent, unstained, separated from sinners and exalted above the heavens. He has no need, like those high priests, to offer sacrifices daily, first for his own sins and then for those of the people, since he did this once for all when he offered up himself. For the law appoints men in their weakness as high priests, but the word of the oath, which came later than the law, appoints a Son who has been made perfect forever. Now the point in what we are saying is this: we have such a high priest, one who is seated at the right hand of the throne of the Majesty in heaven." (Hebrews 7:26-8:1) Jesus, through His death on the cross, did indeed "remove the iniquity of this land in a single day;" He is the Branch.

Prayer:

Jesus, You are the Branch that arose from the stump of Jess; You fulfill all the prophecies and promises of the Old Testament. You did bring righteousness and salvation to us, and You will bring justice to us all. The Branch did become the High Priest, and You gave the final sacrifice, Yourself; the job complete You are sitting on Your throne, glory, and honor are Yours.

The Desire and the Precious of All Nations

> "And I will shake all nations and the desire and the precious things of all nations shall come in, and I will fill this house with splendor, says the Lord of hosts."
> *Haggai 2:7 (AMPC)*

"The desire and the precious...of all nations" is a more difficult name to see at first because of how the English language translates the text and adds the word "things" in the middle. The original text had much debate also due to Chamdath "Desire, Precious," a noun in the singular form being paired with bau, "shall come," a plural verb. Is it speaking of material wealth or the Messiah? The answer is both. As with most prophecies, allusions to the material and spiritual reside in the same place. The ancient Jewish interpreters who rendered this phrase stated that the "tile words, in this case, point to a person; and this person can be no one else than the Messiah for whom all nations consciously or unconsciously yearn, in whom all the longings of the human heart find satisfaction." (Exell and Spence-Jones) Matthew Henry expresses the sentiment this way, "desirable to all nations for in him shall all the earth be blessed with the best of blessings; long expected and desired by all believers... this promise is fulfilled in that spiritual peace which Jesus Christ has by his blood purchased for all believers." (Henry)

Jesus, Precious of All Nations, did come, and He shook all the nations; the world has never been the same. "When the Son of Man comes in his glory, and all the angels with him, then he will sit on his glorious throne. Before him will be gathered all the nations" (Matthew 25:31-31a) His house, His kingdom is filled with His glory.

Prayer:

Thank You, Lord Jesus, for coming, for shaking all the nations. You are the Desire and the Precious of All Nations and my heart's Desire. May all the longings of my heart find satisfaction in You. All nations are before You; let Your kingdom be filled with glory, honor, and praise forever.

Mighty One of Jacob

"And you shall know that I, the Lord, am your Savior and your Redeemer, the Mighty One of Jacob."
Isaiah 60:16b

The Mighty One of Jacob is the combining of two titles, Mighty God and God of Jacob. Jacob refers both to the person Jacob, also known as Israel, and the nation of Israel. The God of Jacob is bound by covenant to protect and deliver His people, Israel, for He is the Mighty God and is the only one who can save and redeem them. Jesus is the Mighty One of Jacob; He fulfills the covenants with Abraham, Isaac, and Jacob, redeeming His people from a debt they could never repay and saving them from eternal damnation through His life, death, and resurrection. "And all the prophets who have spoken, from Samuel and those who came after him, also proclaimed these days. You are the sons of the prophets and of the covenant that God made with your fathers, saying to Abraham, 'And in your offspring shall all the families of the earth be blessed.' God, having raised up his servant, sent him to you first, to bless you by turning every one of you from your wickedness."(Acts 3:24-26) Jesus is the offspring of Abraham, the Mighty One of

Jacob, that turns us from wickedness and gives us the blessings of forgiveness and eternal life.

Prayer:

Mighty One of Jacob, You are our Savior and Redeemer. Jesus, You have delivered Your people from their sins. You have protected them from eternal damnation. You fulfilled Your covenants. You are the Mighty God, the God of Jacob; You are Lord.

Lord of Our Righteousness

> *"In his days Judah will be saved, and Israel will dwell securely. And this is the name by which he will be called: 'The Lord is our righteousness.'"*
> Jeremiah 23:6

"The Lord Our Righteousness is a sweet name to a convinced sinner; to one that has felt the guilt of sin in his conscience, seen his need of that righteousness, and the worth of it." – Matthew Henry

Jesus Christ is the Lord of Our Righteousness. He shed His blood on the cross to atone for our sins; He took the wrath of God that we deserve for those sins and covered us with His perfect righteousness. We are made righteous through faith in His life, death, and resurrection. Jesus exchanges His righteousness for our sin "And because of him you are in Christ Jesus, who became to us wisdom from God, righteousness and sanctification and redemption." (1Corinthians 1:30) "By this name every true believer shall call him, and call upon him. We have nothing to plead but this, Christ has died, yea rather is risen again, and we have taken him for our Lord. This righteousness which he was wrought out to the satisfaction of law and justice, becomes ours; being a free gift given to us, through the Spirit of God, who puts it upon us, clothes us with it, enables us to lay hold upon it, and claim an interest in it." (Henry)

Prayer:

Lord Jesus, You are my Righteousness; only through You am I considered righteous and can dwell securely. Your perfect obedience and complete fulfillment of the Law is the righteous covering through which all grace and mercy are given to me. Your righteousness covers me and allows me to have peace with God. It is the free gift for which I do not have enough words to express my gratitude.

King

"Rejoice greatly, O daughter of Zion! Shout aloud, O daughter of Jerusalem! Behold, your king is coming to you; righteous and having salvation is he, humble and mounted on a donkey, on a colt, the foal of a donkey."
Zechariah 9:9

The King was coming. Zechariah was speaking of the promised King of Israel, the one that David had spoken of, the one that would be from his line and be "righteous and just." (2 Samuel 23:3) The King would bring the Jews salvation; He would set them free from all their oppressors and make them a mighty kingdom. Jesus is that King, except His kingdom is not a temporal, earthly one; His kingdom is eternal. His salvation was not from mere worldly oppression; but from the bondage of sin, death, and hell. Jesus, the King, did come, "They brought the donkey and the colt and put on them their cloaks, and he sat on them. Most of the crowd spread their cloaks on the road, and others cut branches from the trees and spread them on the road. And the crowds that went before him and that followed him were shouting, "Hosanna to the Son of David! Blessed is he who comes in the name of the Lord!

Hosanna in the highest!" (Matthew 21:7-9) A week later, that crowd would be shouting and mocking Jesus as He is beaten and crucified, "And over his head they put the charge against him, which read, "This is Jesus, the King of the Jews." (Matthew 27:37) The people were short-sighted, only thinking of their immediate needs, while the King saw all eternity; "They will make war on the Lamb, and the Lamb will conquer them, for he is Lord of lords and King of kings, and those with him are called and chosen and faithful." (Revelation 17:14)

Prayer:

Jesus, You are the One, True King; You have conquered every foe and vanquished every enemy, including sin, death, and hell forever. You are King of kings; every knee will bow to You one day. Thank You for being righteous and bringing salvation to me. Hosanna in the highest!

Elect One

"Behold! My Servant whom I uphold, My Elect One in whom My soul delights! I have put My Spirit upon Him; He will bring forth justice to the Gentiles."
Isaiah 42:1(NKJV)

Jesus Christ, the Elect One, was chosen "from all eternity in God's counsels to the great work of man's redemption, and to be the Mediator between God and man." (Exell and Spence-Jones) This beautiful prophecy begins to be fulfilled at Jesus' baptism, "And when Jesus was baptized, immediately he went up from the water, and behold, the heavens were opened to him, and he saw the Spirit of God descending like a dove and coming to rest on him, and behold, a voice from heaven said, 'This is my beloved Son, with whom I am well pleased.'" (Matthew 3:16-17) Jesus' death and resurrection, which brings salvation to all who believe in Him, Jew and Gentile alike, complete the prophecy. "But now in Christ Jesus, you who once were far off have been brought near by the blood of Christ. For he himself is our peace, who has made us both one and has broken down in his flesh the dividing wall of hostility...So then you are no longer strangers and aliens, but you are fellow citizens with the saints and members of the household of God." (Ephesians 2:13-19)

Prayer:

Lord Jesus, You are the Elect One, The One in whom the Lord delights. You are the One chosen to show all the love of the Lord to the world. Your life, death, and resurrection bring justice for me, a Gentile, and give me peace and hope.

Arm of the Lord

"Who has believed what he has heard from us? And to whom has the arm of the Lord been revealed?"
    Isaiah 53:1

The arm is an intricate part of how most function. It is a symbol of power, strength, and might. In Scripture, the Arm of the Lord represents the unlimited active power of the Lord. All of Isaiah 53 speaks of the Arm of the Lord being perfectly revealed in Jesus, "in its grandest operation, creation and the continual sustaining of the universe are great, but redemption is greater...The divine power that is enshrined in Jesus' weakness is power in its widest sweep, for it is to everyone that believeth, and in its loftiest purpose, for it is unto salvation." (MacLaren) Jesus' death on the cross, His weakest moment, demonstrated the omnipotence and sovereignty of the Lord. At that moment, the Arm of the Lord bore the wrath all the sins of humanity deserved, defeating sin, death, and hell as He rose again, providing salvation for all who believe in Him. "Oh sing to the Lord a new song, for he has done marvelous things! His right hand and his holy arm have worked salvation for him." (Psalm 98:1)

Prayer:

Arm of the Lord, I do sing praises for the marvelous things You have done. You are my salvation. Thank You that in Your weakest moment on earth, You showed Your power and strength; You have defeated sin and death, giving me eternal life.

Shoot

"There shall come forth a shoot from the stump of Jesse, and a branch from his roots shall bear fruit."
Isaiah 11:1

The image of a tender shoot sprouting from the stump of a fallen tree gives so much hope, the hope of renewal and restoration. Israel needed the hope found in this shoot, as do we all; the people of Israel found themselves dispersed, oppressed, and subjugated by many mighty empires; yet, they could hold on to the hope of "a shoot from the stump of Jesse." The Lord was faithful; they knew He would keep His promise; "And the Spirit of the Lord shall rest upon him, the Spirit of wisdom and understanding, the Spirit of counsel and might, the Spirit of knowledge and the fear of the Lord. And his delight shall be in the fear of the Lord. He shall not judge by what his eyes see, or decide disputes by what his ears hear, but with righteousness, he shall judge the poor, and decide with equity for the meek of the earth; and he shall strike the earth with the rod of his mouth, and with the breath of his lips he shall kill the wicked. Righteousness shall be the belt of his waist, and faithfulness the belt of his loins." (Isaiah 11:2-5) Jesus, whose earthly lineage comes directly from King David, son of Jesse, is the Shoot; His very nature is filled with the Spirit, His judgment righteousness, His character faithfulness; all good fruit comes from Him.

Prayer:

Lord Jesus, the Shoot from the stump of Jesse, we find hope in You. You did not remain a tender shoot but are a mighty tree of life. You are the vigorous, everlasting vine that connects us to the Father. You are our righteousness; You are our everything. You are faithful.

Man of Sorrows

> *"He was despised and rejected by men, a*
> *man of sorrows and acquainted with grief; and*
> *as one from whom men hide their faces he was*
> *despised, and we esteemed him not."*
> *Isaiah 53:3*

Isaiah's prophetic words point to the quintessential element of Jesus' relationship with humankind; He was to suffer on behalf of all humanity. Jesus' entire earthly life was a succession of sorrows and sufferings, from the trials of His existence to the continual flow of people in need of physical healing brought before Him. "That evening, they brought to him many who were oppressed by demons, and he cast out the spirits with a word and healed all who were sick. This was to fulfill what was spoken by the prophet Isaiah: 'He took our illnesses and bore our diseases.'" (Matthew 8:16-17) Jesus' intense love and sympathy made Him feel the pain of others as His own, "When Jesus saw her weeping, and the Jews who had come with her also weeping, he was deeply moved in his spirit and greatly troubled. And he said, "Where have you laid him?" They said to him, "Lord, come and see." Jesus wept. So the Jews said, "See how he loved him!" (John 11:33-36) That same love and sympathy would cause Him to endure the excruciating pain and ultimately death on the cross to save us from the wrath due to us for our sins. "But now the righteousness of God has been manifested apart from the law, although the Law and the Prophets bear witness to it—the righteousness of God through faith in Jesus Christ for all who believe. For there is no distinction: for all have sinned and fall short of the glory of God, and are justified by his grace as a gift, through the redemption that is in Christ Jesus, whom God put forward as a propitiation by his blood, to be received by faith. This was to show God's righteousness because, in his divine forbearance, he had passed over former sins. It was to show his righteousness at the present time so that he might be just and the justifier of the one who has faith in Jesus." (Romans 3:21-26)

Prayer:

Lord Jesus, I am so sorry You had to suffer for my sins; I cannot begin to thank You for all You have done for me. It is Your love, sympathy, and empathy that make You Lord. You can relate to all that I go through, and You love me and care for me despite me being a sinner. You lived as a man of sorrows to prove that love to me.

Messenger of the Covenant

> *"And the Lord whom you seek will suddenly*
> *come to his temple; and the messenger of the cove-*
> *nant in whom you delight, behold, he is coming,*
> *says the Lord of hosts."*
> *Malachi 3:1*

The title Messenger of the Covenant is used only once in Scripture, in this last prophecy spoken through Malachi before four hundred years of silence. The promise of the Messenger of the Covenant is profound. He will be the One who upholds both the Abrahamic Covenant and the Messianic covenant prophesied by Jeremiah and Isaiah. "For this is the covenant that I will make with the house of Israel after those days, declares the Lord: I will put my law within them, and I will write it on their hearts. And I will be their God, and they shall be my people. And no longer shall each one teach his neighbor and each his brother, saying, 'Know the Lord,' for they shall all know me, from the least of them to the greatest, declares the Lord. For I will forgive their iniquity, and I will remember their sin no more." (Jeremiah 31:33-34) Jesus is the Messenger of the Covenant, "Commissioned from his father to bring man home to God by a covenant of grace, who had revolted from him by the violation of the covenant of innocence. By his mediation, this covenant is procured and established; and though he is the prince of the covenant, as some read the clause here, yet he condescended to be the messenger of it, that we might, upon his word, have the fullest assurance of God's goodwill to man." (Benson) Jesus is the One we seek, He did come, and He established a new covenant of grace on the cross. Have you received the Good News of the Messenger of the Covenant?

Prayer:

Lord Jesus, Messenger of the Covenant, thank You for upholding, revealing, and mediating the covenants established by the Lord. You fulfilled the Old Testament's covenants and set a new covenant of grace through Your life, death, and resurrection. Thank You for the grace and mercy You lavish upon me through those covenants.

3

༄

The Names Jesus Gave Himself

The Gospels give an up-close, personal account of Jesus' time on earth, recording what He did and what He said. As Jesus taught, He spoke of Himself in many ways to let those listening know He was the Messiah, the One they had been waiting for, their salvation. Jesus is still revealing Himself through His Word; listen to how He described Himself. He is the One you have been waiting for, Your salvation.

I Am

"Jesus said to them, 'Truly, truly, I say to you, before Abraham was, I am.'"
John 8:58

Jesus boldly declared His divine, eternal existence and His immutable nature, "In the time before Abraham, in the eternity before time, He still was. No word which expresses becoming can be used of His existence." (Ellicott) As Jesus spoke these words to the Jewish crowd, they recalled the Lord saying to Moses, "I am who I am" (Exodus 3:13-14) and through Isaiah, "I am the One" (Isaiah 41:4). Jesus was stating He was Jehovah, YHWH, I Am, and the Jewish crowd was angered and did not believe Him, "So they picked up stones to throw at him, but Jesus hid himself and went out of the temple" (John 8:59).

Do we react the same way as the Jewish crowd? Do we believe Jesus is I am, or do we get angry and wait to throw stones because His answers are not what we expected? Jesus is unchangeable; His love, grace, mercy, faithfulness, His everything invariable. Jesus, I Am, still is, and always will be.

Prayer:

Jesus, You are I Am; You always have been and always will be; You are God. When I do not understand, I react as the Jews did and get angry; but I am so thankful that You never change, that Your love and mercy and grace are not based on my reactions but on Your immutable nature. To I Am goes all praise and glory, Amen.

Bread of Life

"Jesus said to them, 'I am the bread of life; whoever comes to me shall not hunger, and whoever believes in me shall never thirst.'"
John 6:35

Jesus, by naming Himself "the bread of life," is trying to impart the ultimate provision the Lord is providing to those who hear His name. "Truly, truly, I say to you, whoever believes has eternal life. I am the bread of life. Your fathers ate the manna in the wilderness, and they died. This is the bread that comes down from heaven, so that one may eat of it and not die. I am the living bread that came down from heaven. If anyone eats of this bread, he will live forever. And the bread that I will give for the life of the world is my flesh." (John 6:47-51) The people in the Capernaum synagogue had a difficult time understanding the metaphor Jesus was using, and so do we sometimes. Jesus speaks of never being hungry or thirsty (John 6:35), of not dying and eternal life (John 6:40, 47, 50, 58) if we feed on His flesh and eat the bread of life (John 6:49-58).

Even His disciples had a tough time comprehending what He was saying; "When many of his disciples heard it, they said, "This is a hard saying; who can listen to it?" (John 6:60) All of this took place before Jesus' final Passover dinner with the disciples; "Now as they were eating, Jesus took bread, and after blessing it broke it and gave it to the disciples, and said, 'Take, eat; this is my body.' And he took a cup, and when he had given thanks, he gave it to them, saying, 'Drink of it, all of you, for this is my blood of the covenant, which is poured out for many for the forgiveness of sins.'" (Matthew 26:26-28) Yet, the disciples would not understand Jesus' full meaning until after His crucifixion and resurrection; "And the bread that I will give for the life of the world is my flesh." (John 6:51b) Only through Jesus' death and resurrection is eternal life attainable; The Bread of Life sustains us; we do not hunger or thirst, for all our true needs are met in Him. "For this is the will of my Father, that everyone who looks on the Son and believes in him should have eternal life, and I will raise him up on the last day." (John 6:40)

Prayer:

Jesus, Bread of Life, You are all I need to be satisfied, not to hunger or thirst for the things of this world. You gave Your body to bring eternal life with the Lord to me; thank You is not sufficient, but the only words I have to express what is inexpressible gratitude. May I always remember what You have done for me and for the world. Amen

Light of the World

> "*Again Jesus spoke to them, saying, 'I am the light of the world. Whoever follows me will not walk in darkness, but will have the light of life.'*"
> *John 8:12*

Jesus testifies that He is "the light of the world" on the last day of the Feasts of Booths, a festival that commemorates the Israelites' forty-year journey in the wilderness. During that journey, the light of the Lord led them; "And the Lord went before them by day in a pillar of cloud to lead them along the way, and by night in a pillar of fire to give them light, that they might travel by day and by night.The pillar of cloud by day and the pillar of fire by night did not depart from before the people." (Exodus 13:21-22) Jesus, Immanuel, God with us, is the light guiding not just the Israelites but the entire world to the eternal promised land of life with the Lord. Jesus clarifies who God is and the correct path that leads to Him by being light in the darkness. "The true light, which gives light to everyone, was coming into the world." (John 1:9) "In him was life, and the life was the light of men.The light shines in the darkness, and the darkness has not overcome it." (John 1:4-5)

Are you following the Light of the World in your daily journey through the wilderness? Nothing, not even darkness, can overcome Him.

Prayer:

Jesus, Light of the World, thank You for coming to show us the way back to the Lord, for making clear the path that leads to life, both abundant life on earth and eternal life with the Lord. You are the Light that cannot be overcome by darkness; You are the Light of life. Praise God!

Son of Man

"For the Son of Man came to seek and save the lost."
Luke 19:10

Son of Man is a favorite term by which Jesus designates Himself; He uses the name as one that the people would understand to denote the Messiah; therefore, He used it as if it needed no further explanation. "The phrase is more than a mere Hebrew expression to denote man, but is always used with some peculiar characteristic of the person to whom it is applied...it is employed with constant reference to its original meaning to be weak, wick; it is the ethical designation of man...as the phrase "Son of Man" is used in the New Testament when applied by the Savior to Himself, there is an undoubted reference to this fact – that he sustained a peculiar relation to our race; that He was in all respects a man, that He was one of us; that He had so taken our nature on Himself that there was a peculiar propriety that a term which would at once designate that this should be given to Him." (Barnes) Jesus is speaking of Himself as "the Son of Man" since having been born as a human baby, He is entirely man while still being fully God. He is the son of the women, crushing the serpent's seed. (See Genesis 3:15) The prophet Daniel spoke of the Son of Man; "I saw in the night visions, and behold, with the clouds of heaven there came one like a son of man, and he came to the Ancient of Days and was presented before him. And to him was given dominion and glory and a kingdom, that all peoples, nations, and languages should serve him; his dominion is an everlasting dominion, which shall not pass away, and his kingdom one that shall not be destroyed." (Daniel 7:13-14) Jesus confirmed Daniel's prophecy, saying that He would come again, "Then will appear in heaven the sign of the Son of Man, and then all the tribes of the earth will mourn, and they will see the Son of Man coming on the clouds of heaven with power and great glory." (Matthew 24:30) Jesus, the Son of Man, has come and will come again, He is victorious, and His kingdom is everlasting.

Prayer:

Lord Jesus, Son of Man, You came in the form of a baby and grew and lived a sinless life, all to crush the seed of the serpent. You are victorious, You defeat sin, death, and hell, and You will return; Your kingdom has no end. Every people, nation, and tribe will bow to You. Power and glory are Yours.

Bridegroom

"And Jesus said to them, 'Can the wedding guests mourn as long as the bridegroom is with them? The days will come when the bridegroom is taken away from them, and then they will fast.'"

Matthew 9:15

Several times in the Gospels, Jesus refers to the Bridegroom and a wedding feast; the Bridegroom's arrival ends a period of betrothal, of waiting for the promised new relationship to begin. The wedding feast is a joyful time; no one would think of mourning or fasting as long as the bridegroom, the host of the feast, was there. However, the people were not seeing the Bridegroom for who He was and were letting the troubles and hardships of the day ruin the feast. Jesus is our Bridegroom; we are His bride. He has taken care of all the arrangements for the wedding and afterward. He has prepared a place for us. "Let us rejoice and exult and give him the glory, for the marriage of the Lamb has come, and his Bride has made herself ready; it was granted her to clothe herself with fine linen, bright and pure." (Revelation 19:7-8) Jesus, our Bridegroom, took care of everything; His death and resurrection prepared us for this wedding;

His righteousness is what clothed us, making us bright and pure. Do not let the troubles of this day take away the joy of being with the Bridegroom.

Prayer:

My Bridegroom, thank You for making me Your bride and for taking care of all the arrangements. I am sorry I forget that You are with me, and I have no reason to mourn. You have prepared a place for me. I shall rejoice for my Bridegroom is here.

Good Shepherd

"I am the good shepherd. The good shepherd lays down his life for the sheep."
John 10:11

Shepherds were essential in the ancient world; they were to provide food, water, and protection for the flock. Despite having such an important role, they were often considered lowly and dirty, and many did not care for their flocks as they should. Jesus described Himself as the Good Shepherd, using a unique word, *kalos* in Greek, meaning beautiful, noble, wholesome, good. He repeats the phrase several times with the same condition; "I am the good shepherd. I know my own and my own know me, just as the Father knows me and I know the Father; and I lay down my life for the sheep." (John 10:14-15) Jesus did lay down His life for His sheep, dying on the cross, conquering sin and death, and rising on the third day. "For this reason, the Father loves me, because I lay down my life that I may take it up again. No one takes it from me, but I lay it down of my own accord. I have authority to lay it down, and I have authority to take it up again. This charge I have received from my Father." (John 10:17-18) "And he shall stand and shepherd his flock in the strength of the Lord, in the majesty of the name of the Lord his God. And they shall dwell secure, for now he shall be great to the ends of the earth. And he shall be their peace." (Micah 5:4-5a) Only Jesus could be the Good Shepherd.

Prayer:

Lord Jesus, Good Shepherd, You laid down Your life for me. You are mighty and powerful; You have the authority to lay down and take up life and to give life abundantly. You are beautiful and noble. I am secure in You. You are my peace. You shall be great to the ends of the earth and through all eternity.

One Who Sets Free

"Jesus answered them, 'Truly, truly, I say to you, everyone who practices sin is a slave to sin. The slave does not remain in the house forever; the son remains forever. So if the Son sets you free, you will be free indeed.'"
  John 8:34-36

Sin, the tool of the great deceiver, promises fun, fame, and fortune; it even will give it to you for a time but, eventually, leads to a life of slavery. You become enslaved by legalism, tiredness, anger, lies, addiction, or solitude, constantly feeding or fighting the desires that have you bound, never finding the satisfaction or freedom you crave. "For freedom Christ has set us free; stand firm therefore, and do not submit again to a yoke of slavery." (Galatians 5:1) Jesus conquered sin on the cross, fulfilling the law perfectly, atoning for all our sins, and covering us in His righteousness. He is the only one who can set us free. He does so without expecting anything in return; "for all have sinned and fall short of the glory of God, and are justified by his grace as a gift, through the redemption that is in Christ Jesus, whom God put forward as a propitiation by his blood, to be received by faith." (Romans 3:23-25) Jesus, the One Who

Sets Free, offers the freedom that never ends to those who have faith in Him. You do not have to be enslaved, "if the Son sets you free, you will be free indeed."

Prayer:

Jesus, You are the One Who sets us free. You paid the price to redeem us and cover us in Your righteousness. You broke our yoke of slavery. You conquered sin, death, and hell to give us freedom and eternal life with You. Thank You for setting us free.

The Door

> "So Jesus again said to them, 'Truly, truly, I say to you, I am the door of the sheep. All who came before me are thieves and robbers, but the sheep did not listen to them. I am the door. If anyone enters by me, he will be saved and will go in and out and find pasture.'"
> John 10:7-9

Jesus is the Door to salvation, abundant life, and eternal life. Salvation only comes through Jesus Christ; although He was sinless, He bore our sins on the cross and suffered the punishment and death we deserve. Nevertheless, he rose on the third day, having conquered sin, death, and hell, so we may enter into a whole relationship with the Lord and have eternal life. Jesus is the Door by which we enter the throne room of the Lord; it is Jesus' holiness and righteousness that covers us when we accept salvation and join the flock of the Lord. Because Jesus is the Door, no one can steal us from His keeping; the Door cannot be broken or circumvented. We are protected from the eternal effects of sin and death.

Prayer:

Lord Jesus, You are the Door that leads to life. You have provided salvation, and by You, I can enter into a restored relationship with the Lord. As the Door, I can find rest and good pasture through You. You take care of all my needs. You are my protection and provision. Only through You do I have eternal life.

Only Begotten Son

*"For God so loved the world that He gave His
only begotten Son, that whoever believes in Him
should not perish but have everlasting life."
John 3:16 (NKJV)*

While explaining salvation to Nicodemus, Jesus uses this phrase, "only begotten Son," to emphasize who He is and His unique connection to God, the Father. Their relationship goes far beyond any earthly bond of father and child, but it is the closest example to which we can relate. "But all that human thought has ever gathered of tenderness, forgiveness, love, in the relation of father to only child – all this is, in the faintness of an earth-drawn picture, an approach to the true idea of God. Yes, the true idea is infinitely beyond all this; for the love for the world gives in sacrifice the love for the only begotten Son." (Ellicott) Jesus, the Only Begotten Son, is the most profound expression of the love of God for us; He is the Lord's salvation gift to the world.

Prayer:
Lord, I cannot begin to understand the depth of Your love for me as expressed through Jesus, Your Only Begotten Son. I

cannot imagine the pain of seeing Him here and on the cross. Jesus, I am sorry for all You endured on my account. I thank You and praise You for conquering sin and death so that I may live. Thank You, Lord, for Your unfathomable love.

Prophet

"And Jesus said to them, 'A prophet is not without honor, except in his hometown and among his relatives and in his own household.'"
Mark 6:4

"Long ago, at many times and in many ways, God spoke to our fathers by the prophets,but in these last days, he has spoken to us by his Son," Jesus the preeminent Prophet. (Hebrews 1:1-2) Jesus spoke of things to come with all authority and certainty as Emmanuel, God with us; yet, most did not understand or believe what He said when He told of His betrayal, death, and resurrection. Nonetheless, every word Jesus spoke came true.

He also said He would come again, bringing final judgment and redemption; "And then they will see the Son of Man coming in a cloud with power and great glory. Now when these things begin to take place, straighten up and raise your heads because your redemption is drawing near." (Luke 21;27-28) The prophesied words of Jesus are true; hope is found in them, He is coming again. "He (Jesus) who testifies to these things says, "Surely I am coming soon." Amen. Come, Lord Jesus!" (Revelation 22:20)

Prayer:

Come, Lord Jesus, I hold on to the promise that You are coming soon. Your words are true, so hope is found in the prophesied promises You made. Thank You for telling me what the future holds, the good and the bad, so that I may know how the story ends. You are Victorious Emmanuel, Prophet, Priest, and King. Amen, come, Lord Jesus!

Authority

"And Jesus came and said to them, 'All authority in heaven and on earth has been given to me.'"

Matthew 28:18

Authority implies knowledge, wisdom, power, and the right to wield those attributes. Jesus' authority was evident when He spoke; "And when Jesus finished these sayings, the crowds were astonished at his teaching, for he was teaching them as one who had authority, and not as their scribes." (Matthew 7:28-29) The scribes may have had knowledge, but they had no power connected with their teaching. Jesus demonstrated His power and authority over all things as Lord:

"And behold, some people brought to him a paralytic, lying on a bed. And when Jesus saw their faith, he said to the paralytic, 'Take heart, my son; your sins are forgiven.' And behold, some of the scribes said to themselves, 'This man is blaspheming.' But Jesus, knowing their thoughts, said, 'Why do you think evil in your hearts? For which is easier, to say, "Your sins are forgiven," or to say, "Rise and walk"? But that you may know that the Son of Man has authority on earth to forgive sins'—he then said to the paralytic—'Rise, pick up your bed and go home.' And he rose and went home." (Matthew 9:2-7)

Jesus does not just have authority; He is Authority.

Prayer:

Lord Jesus, Authority, You have the power and right to command all things; You are God, Sovereign, Faithful, and in control. You tell the stars when to shine and the seas when to roll. You are the Authority in my life, of my life, and over my life. So I bow to You, Lord Jesus.

Friend

"You are my friends if you do what I command you. No longer do I call you servants, for the servant does not know what his master is doing, but I have called you friends, for all that I have heard from my Father I have made known to you."

John 15:14-15

Jesus chose to be our Friend; "You did not choose me, but I chose you and appointed you that you should go and bear fruit and that your fruit should abide, so that whatever you ask the Father in my name, he may give it to you." (John 15:16) To those who believe and obey Him, He has granted a familiarity far beyond that of a servant; He has brought us into an intimate relationship. He speaks to His friends revealing the Lord's will; "And he answered them, 'To you it has been given to know the secrets of the kingdom of heaven, but to them it has not been given.'" (Matthew 13:11) Jesus personally intercedes for you, to the point of laying down His life for you. "Greater love has no one than this, that someone lay down his life for his friends." (John 15:13) Jesus is the best Friend you can have.

Prayer:

Friend, how great a sentiment to be able to call You, Lord Jesus. You are the One Who called me friend and brought me into a relationship with You. There is no more comforting, loving term than to be called Friend. I love You. Thank You, Jesus, Friend.

True Vine

"I am the true vine, and my Father is the vinedresser."
John 15:1

Jesus, the True Vine, is the vital connection that keeps us tethered to God, the Father; "If anyone does not abide in me he is thrown away like a branch and withers; and the branches are gathered, thrown into the fire, and burned." (John 15:6) He came to provide the way for our relationship with the Father to be restored; so that we do not get thrown away on the day of judgment. Jesus' death and resurrection tore the curtain separating us from the Lord (see Matthew 27:51); His righteousness covers us, and we can approach the Father. Abiding in Jesus gives us all we need to mature and bear fruit; "Abide in me, and I in you. As the branch cannot bear fruit by itself, unless it abides in the vine, neither can you, unless you abide in me." (John 15:4) Abiding does not mean life will be easy; however, it will be more abundant. "Every branch in me that does not bear fruit he takes away, and every branch that does bear fruit he prunes, that it may bear more fruit." (John 15:2) The True Vine empowers us to serve and love one another and be able to glorify the Lord, which we cannot do without Him. "I am the vine; you are the branches. Whoever abides in me and I in him, he it is that bears much fruit. For apart from me, you can do nothing. By this, my Father is glorified, that you bear much fruit and so prove to be my disciples." (John 15:5,8) Even during the pruning seasons, abiding in the True Vine brings us joy. "These things I have spoken to you, that my joy may be in you and that your joy may be full." (John 15:11)

Prayer:

True Vine, You keep me connected to the Father. Jesus, only when I abide in You can I bear fruit; apart from You, I can do nothing. Abiding in You brings abundant life and joy. Let my life in You glorify the Father and bear much fruit; let it prove I am Your disciple. Thank You for being the True Vine and for making my joy-full.

The Resurrection and The Life

"Jesus said to her, 'I am the resurrection and the life. Whoever believes in me, though he die, yet shall he live'"
John 11:25

Jesus confirms His identity, "I am the Resurrection and the Life," while comforting Martha after her brother Lazarus' death. Martha was trusting that Jesus was the Messiah and the resurrection would happen on the last day; yet, Jesus is declaring that Resurrection and Life are a person, Him; "revealing in His own person all that men had ever thought and hoped of a future life, being Himself the power which shall raise them at the last day, and could therefore raise them now." (Ellicott) Being Life, Jesus is the Creator and Sustainer of all life. He alone has the authority to give life. In conjunction, the Resurrection and the Life have complete control over all life and death matters; anyone who believes in Him receives the power to overcome death through Him. Jesus' life, death, and resurrection give all who trust and obey Him eternal life. For followers of Jesus, death is not to be feared; it has no more power over us than sleep; which is how Jesus referred to it when speaking of Lazarus; "After saying these things, he said to them, 'Our friend Lazarus has fallen asleep, but I go to awaken him.'" (John 11:11)

"The believer's death shall be swallowed up in life, and his life shall never sink into death. As death comes by sin, it is His (Jesus) to dissolve it; and as life flows through His righteousness, it is His to communicate and eternally maintain it. (Romans 5:21) The temporary separation of soul and body is here regarded as not even interrupting, much less impairing, the new and everlasting life imparted by Jesus to His believing people." (Jamieson-Fausset-Brown Bible Commentary)

Prayer:

Jesus, Resurrection and Life, how comforting it is to know all life comes from You and that death cannot overcome You. When our earthly lives are done, You give new life, eternal life. Death does not hold You; You are the Resurrection. Praise Jesus, the Resurrection and the Life.

The Way, and the Truth, and the Life

"Jesus said to him, 'I am the way, and the truth, and the life. No one comes to the Father except through me.'"
John 14:6

"Thomas said to him, 'Lord, we do not know where you are going. How can we know the way?'"(John 14:5) It is easy to feel like Thomas in uncertain times, not understanding what the Lord is doing and how we are to follow. Jesus' reply is the same to us as it was to Thomas; "I am the way, and the truth, and the life," to know me is to know the Father and His will. Jesus is the only way to enter the presence of the Lord; His death on the cross atoned for our sins and covered us in His righteousness, restoring our relationship with the Father and giving us eternal life with Him.

Jesus, being fully God, is the Truth. God cannot lie; it is not in His nature; therefore, Jesus cannot lie. As the Truth, through His actions and teachings while on earth; and as the Word (John 1:1) given to us as Scripture, Jesus gives us an accurate understanding of God. Spending time studying the Word, praying, talking to Jesus, developing our relationship with Him leads to abundant life, joy, peace, and purpose in our everyday lives, answering, "How can we know the way?"

Prayer:

Jesus, thank You for being the answer to my biggest questions. You are the Way, the Truth, and the Life; You gave Yourself that I may have a way back to the Father. You are the only way to life because You are Truth. Lord, I love You and praise You for all You are and all You have done.

4

***

Names the Disciples Gave Jesus

The New Testament is filled with the names the disciples ascribed to Jesus, as He revealed Himself to them in person and through the Holy Spirit. They preached and wrote about these names to give a fuller picture of Jesus, who He is, and what He has done; they are names of power, names that tell of His salvation, and names that bring joy and peace. Names that changed the world because they are all names of Jesus.

Lord of All

"Therefore God has highly exalted him and bestowed on him the name that is above every name, so that at the name of Jesus every knee should bow, in heaven and on earth and under the earth, and every tongue confess that Jesus Christ is Lord, to the glory of God the Father."
Philippians 2:9-11

Lord is the most frequently used name for Jesus in the New Testament; yet, it is not a title given to Him by man but bestowed upon Him by God, the Father; "God has highly exalted him and bestowed on him the name that is above every name...Jesus Christ is Lord." Lord, kýrios in Greek, implies absolute ownership rights exercised by a Master or one in authority. When Jesus speaks, "Why do you call me 'Lord, Lord,' and not do what I tell you?" (Luke 6:46) He is not making a polite plea for respect but emphasizes that He is to be obeyed as Master. All authority is given to Jesus; thus, all peoples and powers in the universe are subject to Him; "For if we live, we live to the Lord, and if we die, we die to the Lord. So then, whether we live or whether we die, we are the Lord's. For to this end, Christ died and lived again, that he might be Lord both of the dead and of the living." (Romans 14:8-9) Jesus is Lord; nothing can stand against Him; "They will make war on the Lamb, and the Lamb will conquer them, for he is Lord of lords and King of kings, and those with him are called and chosen and faithful." (Revelation 17:14) Every knee will bow to Jesus, Lord of All.

Prayer:

Lord Jesus, indeed a name above every name, You are Master of all things; and You have authority over all things. You deserve respect, but mostly You deserve to be obeyed. Therefore, Lord, let me be obedient to You and You alone. Thank You that You call me chosen. All glory and honor, and praise are Yours. One day, every knee will bow to You, and every tongue will confess, You are Lord of All.

Propitiation for Our Sins

> "*In this is love, not that we have loved God but that he loved us and sent his Son to be the propitiation for our sins.*"
> *1 John 4:10*

Propitiation can be a scary-sounding "church" word that means to reconcile or appease; it implies making one favorable to turn away the wrath of another. Jesus took the wrath our sins deserve and covered us in His righteousness, making us favorable to God, reconciling our relationship with Him. "We have an advocate with the Father, Jesus Christ the righteous. He is the propitiation for our sins, and not for ours only but also for the sins of the whole world." (1 John 2:1-2) "For all have sinned and fall short of the glory of God, and are justified by his grace as a gift, through the redemption that is in Christ Jesus, whom God put forward as a propitiation by his blood, to be received by faith." (Romans 3:23-25) That scary-sounding word is actually one that begins to show the depth of the love the Lord has for us; "For God so loved the world, that he gave his only Son, that whoever believes in him should not perish but have eternal life. For God did not send his Son into the world to condemn the world, but in order that the world might be saved through him." (John 3:16-17) Oh, how sweet is the name of Jesus, the Propitiation for Our Sins.

Prayer:

Lord Jesus, how thankful I am that You are the Propitiation for my sins; You have reconciled my relationship with the Lord and made me favorable in His sight. You have guaranteed me eternal life through Your righteousness. You are love. You are all I need.

Image of God

"Christ, who is the image of God."
2 Corinthians 4:4

"He (Christ Jesus) is the image of the invisible God, the firstborn of all creation.For by him all things were created, in heaven and on earth, visible and invisible, whether thrones or dominions or rulers or authorities—all things were created through him and for him. And he is before all things, and in him all things hold together. And he is the head of the body, the church. He is the beginning, the firstborn from the dead, that in everything he might be preeminent. For in him all the fullness of God was pleased to dwell, and through him to reconcile to himself all things, whether on earth or in heaven, making peace by the blood of his cross." (Colossians 1:15-20) Jesus Christ is the visible representation of our invisible God; their complete unity within the Trinity means to see One is to see the Other.

Jesus explains this to Philip; "Philip said to him, 'Lord, show us the Father, and it is enough for us.'Jesus said to him, 'Have I been with you so long, and you still do not know me, Philip? Whoever has seen me has seen the Father. How can you say, 'Show us the Father'?Do you not believe that I am in the Father and the Father is in me? The words that I say to you I do not speak on my own authority, but the Father who dwells in me does his works.Believe me that I am in the Father and the Father is in me, or else believe on account of the works themselves.'" (John 14:8-11) We know that Jesus is "Immanuel, God with us;" (Matthew 1:23) hence, He is "the image of God; He is the radiance of the glory of God and the exact imprint of his nature, and he upholds the universe by the word of his power. After making purification for sins, he sat down at the right hand of the Majesty on high." (2 Corinthians 4:4, Hebrews 1:3)

Prayer:

Jesus, You are the beautiful image of God that shows us the love, grace, and mercy of the Lord in living form. You are God with us; there is no other that is God or shows us God the way You do. You are the exact imprint of His nature and how we know the Father. Thank You for being the image of the invisible God and showing us the radiance of His glory.

Deliverer

"And to wait for his Son from heaven, whom he raised from the dead, Jesus who delivers us from the wrath to come."
1 Thessalonians 1:10

"And in this way, all Israel will be saved, as it is written, 'The Deliverer will come from Zion, he will banish ungodliness from Jacob'; 'and this will be my covenant with them when I take away their sins.'" (Romans 11:26-27) The Apostle Paul, in both his letters to the Romans and the Thessalonians, is naming Jesus as our Deliverer. Paul quotes the prophecy of Isaiah (Isaiah 59:20) in his letter to the Romans to prove that Jesus is the Deliverer that came to take away the sins of the people; a point he also emphasizes in his letter to the Thessalonians, that Jesus "delivers us from the wrath to come." Taken together, we can see that Jesus is our Deliverer, past, present, and future; He has already taken on all the wrath and punishment for our sins by being the ultimate sacrifice on the cross. He is delivering us by His intercession and by His grace from the power of sin and temptation. And He will deliver "us from the wrath to come," which is the final judgment; since only through Jesus "who is able to keep you from stumbling and to present you blameless before the presence of his glory with great joy" (Jude 24) are we saved. Therefore, there is hope; no matter what troubles and hardships we face, we have a Deliverer, Jesus Christ the Lord.

Prayer:

Lord Jesus, my Deliverer, I praise You and thank You for all You have done for me. Thank You for saving me from wrath past, present, and future. Thank you for keeping me from stumbling and presenting me blameless before the Lord. You are my Hope and my Deliverer; all praise and glory go to You.

Great High Priest

"Since then we have a great high priest who has passed through the heavens, Jesus, the Son of God, let us hold fast our confession."
Hebrews 4:14

In Old Testament times, the high priest was the only one allowed into the Holy of Holies, the presence of the Lord, to make the atoning sacrifices for the sins of the people in hopes of fulfilling the Law of the Lord; "For every high priest chosen from among men is appointed to act on behalf of men in relation to God, to offer gifts and sacrifices for sins." (Hebrews 5:1) "But when Christ appeared as a high priest of the good things that have come, then through the greater and more perfect tent (not made with hands, that is, not of this creation) he entered once for all into the holy places, not by means of the blood of goats and calves but by means of his own blood, thus securing an eternal redemption." (Hebrews 9:11-12) "For it was indeed fitting that we should have such a high priest, holy, innocent, unstained, separated from sinners, and exalted above the heavens. He has no need, like those high priests, to offer sacrifices daily, first for his own sins and then for those of the people, since he did this once for all when he offered up himself. For the law appoints men in their weakness as high priests, but the word of the oath, which came later than the law, appoints a Son who has been made perfect forever. Now the point in what we are saying is this: we have such a high priest, one who is seated at the right hand of the throne of the Majesty in heaven." (Hebrews 7:26-8:1) Jesus is the Great High Priest, having fulfilled all the duties entirely and perfectly.

Prayer:

Lord Jesus, how thankful I am that You are the Great High Priest fulfilling the law perfectly with Your sacrifice, securing eternal redemption for me and for all who have faith in You. Thank You for being the perfect bridge between the Lord and myself, restoring my relationship with Him. I can hope in You because You have completed Your duties and are seated at the right hand of the throne of Majesty in heaven.

Author of Eternal Salvation

"And having been perfected, He became the
author of eternal salvation to all who obey Him."
Hebrews 5:9 (NKJV)

An author is a source from which something begins, the very cause of its existence. Jesus is the source of eternal salvation; only because of Him does it exist. "We see Jesus, who was made a little lower than the angels, for the suffering of death crowned with glory and honor, that He, by the grace of God, might taste death for everyone. For it was fitting for Him, for whom *are* all things and by whom *are* all things, in bringing many sons to glory, to make the captain of their salvation perfect through sufferings." (Hebrews 2:9-10 NKJV) Jesus lived a human life, faced trials and temptations, suffered and died while remaining sinless, being utterly obedient to God. "In the days of his flesh, Jesus offered up prayers and supplications, with loud cries and tears, to him who was able to save him from death, and he was heard because of his reverence. Although he was a son, he learned obedience through what he suffered." (Hebrews 5:7-8) Jesus' sinless obedience made Him the perfect sacrifice to atone for the sins of the world. His life, death, and resurrection defeated sin, death, and hell, providing "eternal salvation to all who obey Him." Jesus is the Author of Eternal Salvation; praise be to God.

Prayer:

Lord Jesus, You are the Author of Eternal Salvation; only through You is there eternal life with God. You suffered and died to give me life; You paid the debt I could never repay. You are the source of all that I have. You are my hope. To You go all glory and praise.

Indescribable Gift

"Now thanks be to God for His indescribable
gift [which is precious beyond words]!"
2 Corinthians 9:15 (AMP)

Indescribable, unspeakable, and inexpressible are a few ways English translates Paul's outburst of praise. The phrase he uses is found nowhere else in the New Testament; it conveys that the Gift of Jesus cannot be related; "it is higher than the mind can conceive; higher than the language can express." (Barnes) Our human minds just scratch the surface of comprehension regarding the Indescribable Gift that is Jesus Christ. He conquered sin, death, and hell by giving up His heavenly throne, coming to earth as a man, living a sinless life, to be the perfect sacrifice on the cross; then rising again victorious, before taking His seat on His throne at the right hand of the Lord. The grace, mercy, love, and victory that are His alone as our Risen Lord are all encompassed in the Indescribable Gift. The facts are all there; we know them, but we do not begin to fully understand the depth or benefit of all Jesus has done and is doing for us; "even as he chose us in him before the foundation of the world, that we should be holy and blameless before him. In love,he predestined us for adoption to himself as sons through Jesus

Christ, according to the purpose of his will, to the praise of his glorious grace, with which he has blessed us in the Beloved. In him we have redemption through his blood, the forgiveness of our trespasses, according to the riches of his grace, which he lavished upon us, in all wisdom and insight making known to us the mystery of his will, according to his purpose, which he set forth in Christ as a plan for the fullness of time, to unite all things in him, things in heaven and things on earth." (Ephesians 1:4-10) Paul was right; Jesus is the Indescribable Gift.

Consider the Gift that is Jesus; what words do you use to describe Him? Now consider that those words barely scratch the surface of who Jesus is; praise Jesus, the Indescribable Gift.

Prayer:

Lord Jesus, Indescribable Gift, I do not begin to comprehend all You have done for me. You gave Your life so that I may have eternal life with You. You have covered me in the grace and mercy of Your righteousness. No earthly language can convey the free gift You have given me. You have blessed me and lavished upon me the riches of Your grace. All honor and glory are Yours.

Our Hope

"Paul, an apostle of Christ Jesus by command
of God our Savior and of Christ Jesus our hope"
1 Timothy 1:1

All hope is found in Jesus. He is the ground on which every hope rests and emanates; without Jesus, there is no hope, no surety of a future, no salvation. Only through the shedding of Jesus' blood to atone for the sin of the world, and His resurrection, by which sin and death were conquered, is hope; confident, unfailing Hope, given. "And not only the creation, but we ourselves, who have the first fruits of the Spirit, groan inwardly as we wait eagerly for adoption as sons, the redemption of our bodies. For in this hope, we were saved." (Romans 8:23-24) Jesus has restored our relationship with the Lord; He has guaranteed us eternal life with Him. He is our salvation, our Hope. "We have this as a sure and steadfast anchor of the soul, a hope that enters into the inner place behind the curtain, where Jesus has gone as a forerunner on our behalf, having become a high priest forever after the order of Melchizedek." (Hebrews 6:19-20) Tikvah is the Hebrew word from which "Hope" is derived; unlike its English counterpart, which is akin to wishing for something to happen, Tikvah implies a firm, confident expectation of what is to come. Even more interestingly, Tikvah can be defined as a cord or rope; our Hope, our rope, is binding us to the most significant, most vital, most secure, everlasting never-failing anchor there is, Jesus Christ. Have you put your hope in Jesus? He is the only Hope that is sure, steadfast, and saves.

Prayer:

Christ Jesus, my Hope, every hope I have is found in You. Without You, every longing would be just a wish floating in the wind. In You, abundant life is found, joy and peace overflow. In You, eternal life is promised; new life with no more pain and no more tears; You are Hope, the sure and steadfast anchor of my soul.

Advocate

*"My little children, I am writing these
things to you so that you may not sin. But if
anyone does sin, we have an advocate with the
Father, Jesus Christ the righteous."*
1 John 2:1

An advocate speaks in defense of another, willing to plead
their case as it is their own. Jesus is our Advocate with the
Father; He is the "one who speaks to the Father in our defense."
(1 John 2:1 NIV) He is the Righteous One through whom we
can approach the Father because "He is the propitiation of our
sins, and nor for ours only but also for the sins of the whole
world." (1 John 2:2) Jesus took on all sin – yours, mine, everyone's throughout all time – while on the cross; His innocent,
sinless blood was the perfect sacrifice to atone for sin; His
death and resurrection defeated sin, saving us from its eternal
damnation. "If we confess our sins, he is faithful and just to
forgive us our sins and to cleanse us from all unrighteousness."
(1 John 1:9) While we are in this broken, sin-filled world, we
will still sin; but, through Jesus, our Advocate, we have hope;
He is faithful and just; He has covered us in His righteousness.
"Beloved, we are God's children now, and what we will be has

not yet appeared; but we know that when he appears, we shall be like him because we shall see him as he is. And everyone who thus hopes in him purifies himself as he is pure." (1 John 3:2-3)

Prayer:

Lord Jesus, it is excellent to know that You are my Advocate; You have pleaded my case before the Father, and I am declared innocent because of Your blood and righteousness covering me. Thank You for standing between the Father and me, for restoring my relationship with him, allowing me to become one of God's children. All hope is found in You, amen.

Holy One of God

"Simon Peter answered him, 'Lord, to whom shall we go? You have the words of eternal life, and we have believed, and have come to know, that you are the Holy One of God.'"
John 6:68-69

Holy is a term that can only honestly describe the Lord. The Hebrew word for holy, "godesh," implies sacredness and apartness, while the Greek, hagios, means pure, morally blameless, and set apart; together, they show that God is altogether different from us. Jesus being God maintained His holiness as a man to be the Holy One of God, the Messiah bringing salvation and eternal life to those who believe and follow Him. The title and its attributes are who Jesus is; whether one follows Him or not, as the demons acknowledge; "And immediately there was in their synagogue a man with an unclean spirit. And he cried out, "What have you to do with us, Jesus of Nazareth? Have you come to destroy us? I know who you are—the Holy One of God." (Mark 1:23-24)

Prayer:

Holy One of God, You are set apart; You are sacred and pure. You remained innocent and blameless, even as they crucified You, to be able to give eternal life to those who follow You. Therefore, all of heaven and earth declare You are the Holy One of God.

Rock

"and all drank the same spiritual drink. For they drank from the spiritual Rock that followed them, and the Rock was Christ."
1 Corinthians 10:4

Paul reminds the Corinthians, and all Christ-follower, of the Lord's provision for their forefathers as they wandered in the wilderness, stating that Jesus Christ was that provision then and that He is even more so now. Just as the Lord provided water from the rock in the desert to sustain the people; He now, through Jesus, the Rock, says, "whoever drinks of the water that I will give him will never be thirsty again. The water that I will give him will become in him a spring of water welling up to eternal life." (John 4:14) The title of the Rock would also bring to mind the songs of King David; "The Lord is my rock and my fortress and my deliverer, my God, my rock, in whom I take refuge, my shield, and the horn of my salvation, my stronghold." (Psalm 18:2) "For God alone my soul waits in silence; from him comes my salvation. He alone is my rock and my salvation, my fortress; I shall not be greatly shaken." (Psalm 62:1-2) "Blessed be the Lord, my rock, who trains my hands for war, and my fingers for battle; he is my steadfast love and my fortress, my stronghold and my deliverer, my shield and he in whom I take refuge." (Psalm 144:1-2) The assurance of these songs is found in Jesus, the Rock; salvation, deliverance, steadfast love, and eternal life come only through Jesus. He is the refuge, the stronghold, the Rock on which all Believers stand. Jesus promised, "Everyone then who hears these words of mine and does them will be like a wise man who built his house on the rock. And the rain fell, and the floods came, and the winds blew and beat on that house, but it did not fall, because it had been founded on the rock." (Matthew 7:24-25) "And the Rock was Christ"!

Prayer:

Lord Jesus, You are the Rock on which I stand. When the storms of life come, I can take refuge in You, in Your salvation, and know that I will not be greatly shaken. You have given me eternal life as the living water welling inside me; I will never be thirsty again. Your steadfast love has delivered me!

Peace

"For he himself is our peace, who has made us both one and has broken down in his flesh the dividing wall of hostility."
Ephesians 2:14

Jesus Christ is Peace; He is not only the bringer and giver of peace, His very nature as Lord is peace; Jehovah Shalom. Just as with Gideon, the Lord says to us; "Peace be to you. Do not fear; you shall not die." (Judges 6:24) Jesus is peace between God and man. "And you, who were dead in your trespasses and the uncircumcision of your flesh, God made alive together with him, having forgiven us all our trespasses, by canceling the record of debt that stood against us with its legal demands. This he set aside, nailing it to the cross." (Colossians 2:13-14) "Therefore, since we have been justified by faith, we have peace with God through our Lord Jesus Christ." (Romans 5:1) Jesus' death and resurrection mean we have nothing to fear; He has defeated sin and death. Our debt of unrighteousness has been paid by Jesus' blood, breaking down the walls that stood between the Lord and us.

Jesus is also Peace for humankind; only through Jesus Christ is there unity of nation, tongue, and tribe. "So then you are no longer strangers and aliens, but you are fellow citizens with the saints and members of the household of God, built on the foundation of the apostles and prophets, Christ Jesus himself being the cornerstone, in whom the whole structure, being joined together, grows into a holy temple in the Lord. In him, you also are being built together into a dwelling place for God by the Spirit." (Ephesians 2:19-22) "Put on then, as God's chosen ones, holy and beloved, compassionate hearts, kindness, humility, meekness, and patience, bearing with one another and, if one has a complaint against another, forgiving each other; as the Lord has forgiven you, so you also must forgive. And above all these put on love, which binds everything together in perfect harmony. And let the peace of Christ rule in your hearts, to which indeed you were called in one body. And be thankful." (Colossians 3:12-13) Jehovah Shalom.

Prayer:

Jesus, You are Peace, Jehovah Shalom. In You, all peace is found; no matter what I face, I know that You have justified me before the Lord, and there is no longer any hostility between us. Lord Jesus, let the Your peace rule my heart, letting kindness, humility, meekness, and patience grow in my life. Thank You that Your Peace and love bind everything together. Amen.

Holy and Righteous One

> *"But you denied the Holy and Righteous One,*
> *and asked for a murderer to be granted to you,"*
> *Acts 3:14*

Peter makes this declaration after he and John, through Jesus' name and the power of the Holy Spirit, heal a lame man. Peter explains to the crowd how the healing had taken place: through Jesus, the Holy and Righteous One, and His power in which the miracle was done, not through any of their abilities. Peter emphasized Jesus' divine, moral perfection by using titles found throughout Hebrew Scriptures that belonged to the Lord and to the Messiah to get the crowd's attention. "For I am God and not a man, the Holy One in your midst, and I will not come in wrath." (Hosea 11:9) "The Lord within her (Jerusalem) is righteous; He does no injustice." (Zephaniah 3:5) "Let the counsel of the Holy One of Israel draw near, and let it come, that we may know it." (Isaiah 5:19) "Out of the anguish of his soul he shall see and be satisfied; by his knowledge shall the righteous one, my servant, make many to be accounted righteous, and he shall bear their iniquities." (Isaiah 53:11)

Having their attention, Peter then gives the charge; "But what God foretold by the mouth of all the prophets, that his

Christ would suffer, he thus fulfilled. Repent, therefore, and turn back, that your sins may be blotted out." (Acts 3:18-19) The Lord had provided salvation through Christ Jesus, the Holy and Righteous One; the people just had to recognize and accept it, as do we.

Prayer:

Holy and Righteous One, You are the Messiah, the One who brings salvation. Do not let us be like the people Peter was admonishing; we do not want to deny You but to know You the way Peter did. Your righteousness covers us, and You bore all our iniquities. Therefore, we repent; salvation is through You alone, Holy and Righteous One.

Intercessor

"Consequently, he (Jesus) is able to save to the uttermost those who draw near to God through him, since he always lives to make intercession for them."
Hebrews 7:25

An Intercessor is a person of influence and power pleading your cause; Jesus Christ is our Intercessor. The book of Hebrews is all about how Jesus is uniquely and ideally suited to be our intercessor with God, the Father. Jesus is the one God promised; "Yet it was the will of the Lord to crush him; he has put him to grief; when his soul makes an offering for guilt, he shall see his offspring; he shall prolong his days; the will of the Lord shall prosper in his hand. Out of the anguish of his soul, he shall see and be satisfied; by his knowledge shall the righteous one, my servant, make many to be accounted righteous, and he shall bear their iniquities. Therefore I will divide him a portion with the many, and he shall divide the spoil with the strong, because he poured out his soul to death and was numbered with the transgressors, yet he bore the sin of many, and makes intercession for the transgressors." (Isaiah 53:10-12) "For it was indeed fitting that we should have such a high priest, holy, innocent, unstained, separated from sinners, and exalted above the heavens. He has no need, like those high priests, to offer sacrifices daily, first for his own sins and then for those of the people, since he did this once for all when he offered up himself." (Hebrews7:26-27) Only Jesus Christ can do these things; He stands in the gap between God and us and intercedes by His life, death, and resurrection. We have nothing to fear; through Jesus, we are reconciled to God and cannot be separated from Him. "Who shall bring any charge against God's elect? It is God who justifies. Who is to condemn? Christ Jesus is the one who died—more than that, who was raised—who is at the right hand of God, who indeed is interceding for us." (Romans 8:33-34)

Prayer:

Lord Jesus, how comforting it is to know that You are my Intercessor; You are the One pleading my case before the Lord. Your sacrifice makes me righteous before Him, You have justified me, and I can trust in You. No one can bring any charge against me because you are interceding for me.

Blessed and Only Sovereign

> "To keep the commandment unstained and free from reproach until the appearing of our Lord Jesus Christ, which he will display at the proper time—he who is the blessed and only Sovereign, the King of kings and Lord of lords."
> 1 Timothy 6:14-15

As Paul closes his letter to Timothy, he emphatically names Jesus "the blessed and only Sovereign," the mighty Ruler with ultimate power over everything. He is "our blessed hope;" (Titus 2:13) the One from whom all blessings flow. Jesus is deserving of this title because "God has highly exalted him and bestowed on him the name that is above every name, so that at the name of Jesus every knee should bow, in heaven and on earth and under the earth, and every tongue confess that Jesus Christ is Lord, to the glory of God the Father." (Philippians 2:9-11) Jesus is Blessed; He is Sovereign, above all things, and He is with us, "Behold, I am with you always, to the end of the age." (Matthew 28:20)

Prayer:

Blessed and Sovereign Lord Jesus, I praise Your name; You are in control of everything, and every nation and tribe will bow to You. You are the name above every name, Jesus, to You goes all honor and glory forever. Amen.

Our Passover Lamb

"For Christ, our Passover lamb, has been sacrificed."
1 Corinthians 5:7

Jesus, "the Lamb of God" (John 1:29), is our perfect Passover lamb; He was without blemish, living a sinless life. Jesus was pure and innocent, not tainted by the world's brokenness; yet, He was slain to make atonement for our sins. His blood causes the wrath of God, the angel of death, to pass over us, just as the lamb's blood did during the last plague of Egypt. Jesus was sacrificed as our Passover lamb. His sacrifice was the last one that would need to be made; "And by that will we have been sanctified through the offering of the body of Jesus Christ once for all. And every priest stands daily at his service, offering repeatedly the same sacrifices, which can never take away sins. But when Christ had offered for all time a single sacrifice for sins, he sat down at the right hand of God, waiting from that time until his enemies should be made a footstool for his feet. For by a single offering he has perfected for all time those who are being sanctified." (Hebrews 10:10-14) Our Passover Lamb conquered sin, death, and hell; "Worthy are you to take the scroll and to open its seals, for you were slain, and by your blood, you ransomed people for God from every tribe and language and people and nation, and you have made them a kingdom and priests to our God, and they shall reign on the earth." Then I looked, and I heard around the throne and the living creatures and the elders the voice of many angels, numbering myriads of myriads and thousands of thousands, saying with a loud voice, "Worthy is the Lamb who was slain, to receive power and wealth and wisdom and might and honor and glory and blessing!" (Revelation 5:9-12)

Prayer:

Lord Jesus, Our Passover Lamb, You are worthy of all blessings, honor, power, and glory forever. Thank You for taking the wrath of God and letting it pass over those who believe and obey You. Thank You for conquering sin, death, and hell. Lamb of God, Lord Jesus, thank You for being our perfect Passover Lamb.

Prince of Life

"and killed the Prince of Life, whom God raised from the dead, of which we are witnesses."
Acts 3:15 (NKJV)

The rendering used here for "Prince" denotes the first person in order, the leader of that which the title is attached. Jesus is the Prince of Life; all life, be it temporal or eternal, begins with Him; "All things were made through him, and without him was not any thing made that was made. In him was life, and the life was the light of men" (John 1:3-4) "And this is the testimony, that God gave us eternal life, and this life is in His Son. Whoever has the Son has life; whoever does not have the Son of God does not have life." (1 John 5:11-12) Jesus is the Creator and Giver of abundant life; He is the only way to eternal life in heaven; "Jesus said to him, 'I am the way, and the truth, and the life. No one comes to the Father except through me.'" (John 14:6) Jesus is the Prince of Life.

Prayer:
Lord Jesus, You are the Prince of Life; all life comes from You and is in You. You are Creator, creating and giving life to everything in existence. Only through You can we gain access

to the Father. You are the One who gives eternal life in heaven. You are the Way and the Truth and the Life; Lord Jesus, thank You for being the Prince of Life.

Lord of Glory

"None of the rulers of this age understood this, for if they had, they would not have crucified the Lord of glory."
1 Corinthians 2:8

"Lord of Glory" refers to Jesus' divine nature; as Lord, He possesses all glory, and all honor and glory are due to Him. The expression is taken from Psalm 24:8-10 to emphasize the ignorance of the rulers and their actions in crucifying Jesus. "Who is this King of glory? The Lord, strong and mighty, the Lord, mighty in battle! Lift up your heads, O gates! And lift them up, O ancient doors, that the King of glory may come in. Who is this King of glory? The Lord of hosts, he is the King of glory!" Jesus, through His life, death, and resurrection, removes the veil allowing us to see the glory of the Lord; "But their minds were hardened. For to this day, when they read the old covenant, that same veil remains unlifted because only through Christ is it taken away. Yes, to this day, whenever Moses is read, a veil lies over their hearts. But when one turns to the Lord, the veil is removed. Now the Lord is the Spirit, and where the Spirit of the Lord is, there is freedom. And we all, with unveiled faces, beholding the glory of the Lord, are being transformed into the same image from one degree of glory to another. For this comes from the Lord who is the Spirit." (2 Corinthians 3:14-18)

Prayer:

Lord of Glory, You are strong and mighty. Lift up our heads that we may see You and understand who You are. Transform us; we want to see You with unveiled faces. Thank You, Jesus, for removing the veil and giving us freedom. All honor and praise go to the Lord of Glory.

Mediator

"For there is one God, and there is one mediator between God and men, the man Christ Jesus,"
1 Timothy 2:5

A mediator is a go-between attempting to resolve conflict among two or more parties. Jesus is the "one mediator between God and men;" His life, death, and resurrection provided the resolution required to reconcile the relationship between God and man. "For while we were still weak, at the right time Christ died for the ungodly; therefore, since we have been justified by faith, we have peace with God through our Lord Jesus Christ." (Romans 5:6, 5:1) Jesus "Is the mediator of a new covenant, so that those who are called may receive the promised eternal inheritance since a death has occurred that redeems them from the transgressions committed under the first covenant." (Hebrews 9:15) On the cross, Jesus took the wrath of God; He shed His perfect, sinless blood to atone for the sins of all humankind, paying the price to redeem us from our transgressions. Through His acts of mediation, all who have faith in Him are justified, made just as if they never sinned, and have peace with God, guaranteeing eternal life with Him.

Prayer:

Lord Jesus, the one Mediator between God and man, thank You for resolving the conflict of sin, defeating sin and death, and bringing me justification and peace. Thank You for being the go-between, the only one who stands in the gap between God and me. You are my Mediator, and through You, I have eternal life and peace with God.

Head of the Church

"And he put all things under his feet and gave him as head over all things to the church, which is his body, the fullness of him who fills all in all."
Ephesians 1:22-23

Jesus is the Head of the Church, "which is his body." Throughout the New Testament, followers of Christ, the church, are referred to as the body of Christ, "For as in one body we have many members, and the members do not all have the same function, so we, though many are one body in Christ, and individually members one of another" (Romans 12:4-5) "We are to grow up in every way into him who is the head, into Christ, from whom the whole body is joined and held together by every joint with which it is equipped." (Ephesians 4:15-16) God, the Father, "put all things under his feet" as "all things were created through him and for him. And he is before all things, and in him all things hold together. And he is the head of the body, the church. He is the beginning, the firstborn from the dead, that in everything he might be preeminent." (Colossians 1:16-18)

Prayer:

Lord Jesus, You are the Head of the Church; as believers, everything we do flows from You. You are the person that unites us throughout all time and space. You give us purpose, to grow in You; You provide us with the mission to share Your Gospel; let us be Your body, Head of the Church. Jesus, You are preeminent in all things; all glory and honor are Yours forever.

Founder and Perfecter of Our Faith

> *"Looking to Jesus, the founder and perfecter of our faith, who for the joy that was set before him endured the cross, despising the shame, and is seated at the right hand of the throne of God."*
> *Hebrews 12:2*

Founder and Perfecter are distinguished titles meant to set Jesus apart from the faithful listed previously in Hebrews 11. Jesus is not only the preeminent example of faith but also the Founder of it. We center our faith on the source, Jesus; "it will be counted to us who believe in him who raised from the dead Jesus our Lord, who was delivered up for our trespasses and raised for our justification. Therefore, since we have been justified by faith, we have peace with God through our Lord Jesus Christ. Through him, we have also obtained access by faith into this grace in which we stand, and we rejoice in hope of the glory of God." (Romans 4:24-25) Jesus is the Perfecter of our faith, "for all the promises of God find their Yes in him. That is why it is through him that we utter our Amen to God for his glory. And it is God who establishes us with you in Christ, and has anointed us, and who has also put his seal on us and given us his Spirit in our hearts as a guarantee." (2 Corinthians 1:20-21) We can abide in the Founder and Perfecter of our faith because he did endure the cross and was victorious over sin, death, and hell, and is now "seated at the right hand of the throne of God." Do you find your "Yes" and "Amen" in the Founder and Perfecter of your faith?

Prayer:

Lord Jesus, how wonderful it is to know that You are seated on Your throne, that You have been victorious over sin and death; therefore, my faith is found and perfected in You. You are the source of faith and my anchor to hope. Thank You for being the Founder and Perfecter of my faith. In You, all the promises of God find their Yes and Amen.

Heir of All Things

"but in these last days, He has spoken to us by His Son, whom He has appointed the heir of all things, through whom also He created the world."

Hebrews 1:2

The law of inheritance rights was fundamental in Biblical times; having an heir, a son, would guarantee a family's legacy. According to the inheritance rights, the first-born son would be given all authority over the family and its possessions as an heir. Therefore, establishing Jesus as the Heir of All Things is essential in the letter to the Hebrews. Jesus is the Son of God, "He is the radiance of the glory of God and the exact imprint of his nature, and he upholds the universe by the word of his power. After making purification for sins, he sat down at the right hand of the Majesty on high." (Hebrews1:3) Jesus possesses all inheritance rights not only as Son, but as Creator and Redeemer as well. (See Hebrews 1:8-12) Thusly, "all things within the compass of God; all that God is, all that God hath, all that God can or will do; all dominions of God; heaven, earth, and hell, are His." (Poole) Jesus has been given authority because He is the Heir of All Things.

Prayer:

Lord Jesus, Heir of All Things, You are the Son of God, Creator, and Redeemer of all life; everything belongs to You. You are seated at the Father's right hand, and everything bows at Your feet. All glory and honor are Yours.

Judge

*"And he commanded us to preach to the
people and to testify that he is the one appointed
by God to be judge of the living and the dead."*
Acts 10:42

Jesus is the One appointed by God, the Father, to preside over final judgment. Jesus spoke of judgment day and of His authority to judge; "Truly, truly, I say to you, an hour is coming and is now here when the dead will hear the voice of the Son of God, and those who hear will live For as the Father has life in himself, so he has granted the Son also to have life in himself. And he has given him authority to execute judgment because he is the Son of Man." (John 5:25-27) Jesus' divinity and humanity make Him the perfect Judge; His life, death, and resurrection prove that judgment is coming; "Being then God's offspring, we ought not to think that the divine being is like gold or silver or stone, an image formed by art and imagination of man. The times of ignorance God overlooked, but now he commands all people everywhere to repent because he has fixed a day on which he will judge the world in righteousness by a man whom he has appointed, and of this, he has given assurance to all by raising Him from the dead." (Acts

17:29-31) Jesus is righteous, holy, fair, and equitable, searching the hearts of man and understanding their motives. Jesus is Lord. He is Truth; He is the only One trustworthy to be right; Jesus is Judge.

Prayer:

Lord Jesus, You are the only One worthy to be Judge; You are holy and righteous, trustworthy in all things. You are just and fair. Only You know the intentions of the hearts of man; You cannot be deceived. You have conquered sin and death. You are on the great white throne presiding overall. You are our Judge; glory and honor are Yours.

Overseer of Your Souls

> *"He himself bore our sins in his body on the tree, that we might die to sin and live to righteousness. By his wounds you have been healed. For you were straying like sheep but have now returned to the Shepherd and Overseer of your souls."*
> *1 Peter 2:24-25*

Your soul, that part of you that makes you, you; that part you do not understand completely, that part that is eternal, has an Overseer, Jesus, who fully understands your soul's unique, eternal nature. The affection conveyed within the title of Overseer of your soul "implies that the soul is the special care of the Savior, that it is the object of his special interest; and that it is of great value – so great that it is that which mainly deserves regard." (Barnes) That love is overwhelming; the Good Shepherd (John 10:11), He is our Guardian (as some translate), He comes after us when we stray. (see Luke 15:3-7) The sin of this world no longer taints your soul; it has been made righteous and whole by Jesus, which is enough to deserve the title of Overseer of your soul, but it does not end there. "Consequently, he is able to save t the uttermost those who draw near to God through him, since he always lives to make intercession for them." (Hebrews 7:25) Jesus is still overseeing the care of your soul, interceding for you, guarding your soul against all that may come against it. "Who shall separate us from the love of Christ? Shall tribulation, or distress, or persecution, or famine, or nakedness, or danger, or sword? No, in all these things, we are more than conquerors through him who loved us. For I am sure that neither death nor life, nor angels nor rulers, nor things present nor things to come, nor powers, nor height nor depth, nor anything else in all creation, will be able to separate us from the love of God in Christ Jesus our Lord." (Romans 8:35,37-39) We have nothing to fear; Jesus is the Overseer of our soul.

Prayer:

Lord Jesus, Overseer of my soul, nothing can separate me from You, Praise God! I have nothing to fear; You are my Guardian and Protector. You have saved me from sin and death. You take special care of my soul. You have given me eternal life. Thank You for being the Overseer of my soul.

Holy Servant

"For truly in this city there were gathered together against your holy servant Jesus, whom you anointed, both Herod and Pontius Pilate, along with the Gentiles, and the people of Israel."
Acts 4:27

"The Son of Man came not to be served but to serve, and to give his life as a ransom for many." (Matthew 20:28) The world celebrates fame, power, and position; Jesus revealed that the Lord treasures different qualities; obedience and servanthood. Jesus, being God, knew He was coming to suffer and die, "out of the anguish of his soul he shall see and be satisfied; by his knowledge shall the righteous one, my servant, make many to be accounted righteous, and shall bear their iniquities." (Isaiah 53:11) He understood that even though He is Lord, Holy and Righteous, He is also the Anointed, obedient servant of the Lord's will. In His humanness, He prayed, "My Father, if it be possible, let this cup pass from me; nevertheless, not as I will but as You will." (Matthew 26:29) Three times Jesus prayed and voiced His human desire while seeking and surrendering to the Lord's perfect will. There was no other way. Being the obedient, Holy Servant, Jesus served the world, including those gathered against Him, by bearing our iniquities on the cross. He shed His blood to atone for our sin, covering us in His righteousness. By rising again, Jesus destroyed sin and death forever. "Consequently, he is able to save to the uttermost those who draw near to God through him, since he always lives to make intercession for them." (Hebrews 7:25)

Prayer:

Jesus, Holy Servant, thank You for being obedient and humble; for serving by suffering so that I may live. You conquered sin and death through Your obedience. Lord Jesus, teach me to follow Your example to serve instead of being served. Holy Servant, You are exalted and reign forever.

Grace of God

"For the grace of God has appeared, bringing salvation for all people."
Titus 2:11

"Grace is the shorthand word for the self-motived, ever-acting, communicating, and stooping love which brings in its hands the gift of forgiveness, and deals with those on whom it lavishes this tenderness, not according to their merits, but according to the pulsations of its own heart...which has its very home and throne in the heart of God Himself." (MacLaren) Grace, the free, unconditional, unmerited favor of God, is the foundation of the redemptive, restorative salvation of Jesus Christ. God's grace became visible in the person of Jesus; His life, death, and resurrection bring the free gift of salvation to all that believe in Him. Only through the Grace of God, Jesus, are sinners made righteous before God, the relationship between God and man restored. "God shows his love for us in that while we were still sinners, Christ died for us." (Romans 5:8) We did not and cannot earn our salvation, nor can we lose it, due to the Grace of God; "according to the purpose of his will, to the praise of his glorious grace, with which he has blessed us in the Beloved. In him, we have redemption through his blood, the forgiveness of our trespasses, according to the riches of his grace, which he lavished upon us, in all wisdom and insight, making know to us the mystery of his will, according to his purpose, which he set forth in Christ." (Ephesians 1:5-9) Does acknowledging Jesus by His name, Grace of God, change how you view Him? Does it give you a better understanding of the love and forgiveness lavished upon you?

Prayer:

Lord Jesus, You are the Grace of God lavished upon me. Your righteousness covers me; You restored me to the Lord. You are redeeming my story; I cannot earn my salvation; You have given it to me freely. And I cannot lose it, all because of You, Grace of God. Thank You! All glory and praise to You. Amen

5

❧

Revelatory Names

The triumphant, powerful names of Jesus found in the book of Revelation give hope beyond measure. Each name or title conveys the immutable might and love of Jesus Christ; they speak of His victory over sin, death, and hell, and the promise of eternal life with Him when He returns.

Faithful Witness

"and from Jesus Christ the faithful witness, the firstborn of the dead, and the ruler of kings on earth."
Revelation 1:5

Jesus spoke of being the faithful witness, "You say that I am a king. For this purpose I was born and for this purpose, I have come into the world—to bear witness to the truth. Everyone who is of the truth listens to my voice." (John 18:37) He is the promised offspring: "Once for all, I have sworn by my holiness; I will not lie to David. His offspring shall endure forever, his throne as long as the sun before me. Like the moon, it shall be established forever, a faithful witness in the skies." (Psalm 89:35-37) Jesus testified, "For the works that the Father has given me to accomplish, the very works that I am doing, bear witness about me that the Father has sent me. And the Father who sent me has himself borne witness about me." (John 5:36-37) As the Faithful Witness, Jesus "has freed us from our sins by his blood and made us a kingdom, priests to His God and Father." (Revelation 1:5-6) Therefore, He "is faithful in the sense that He is the one on whose testimony there may be entire reliance." (Barnes) Jesus is entirely worthy of belief; thus, we can find all hope in Him.

Prayer:

Jesus, You are the Faithful Witness, all You say is true and trustworthy. I can have hope because You have promised eternal life to all who follow You. You have freed me from the penalty of sin and made me part of Your kingdom. Thank You, Lord Jesus, for being the Faithful Witness.

The Alpha and The Omega

"I am the Alpha and the Omega," says the Lord God, "who is and who was and who is to come, the Almighty."
Revelation 1:8

Alpha and Omega are the first and last letters of the Greek alphabet; they denote the eternity and divinity of the one they are being applied to. The Lord is, without a doubt, the One "who is and who was and who is to come." The title also represents the perfection and completion of all things in the Lord Jesus Christ. In Jesus, "All things were made through him, and without him was not anything made that was made." (John 1:3) And through Jesus all things are completed; "And he said to me, "It is done! I am the Alpha and the Omega, the beginning and the end. To the thirsty, I will give from the spring of the water of life without payment." (Revelation 21:6) Salvation comes only from the Lord Jesus Christ. He is the beginning and end of salvation, which is why He tells us, "I, Jesus, have sent my angel to testify to you about these things for the churches. Behold, I am coming soon, bringing my recompense with me, to repay each one for what he has done. I am the

Alpha and the Omega, the first and the last, the beginning and the end." (Revelation 22:16, 12-13)

Prayer:
Lord Jesus, You are the Alpha and the Omega, the beginning and the end of all things, nothing exists apart from You, and in You, all things are completed and made perfect. Come, Lord Jesus! Amen.

The Almighty

"I am the Alpha and the Omega," says the Lord God, "who is and who was and who is to come, the Almighty."
Revelation 1:8

The Almighty, referring to the Lord Jesus Christ, occurs nine times in the book of Revelation to show that He is Jehovah Sabaoth, Lord of Hosts, commanding all the hosts and armies of heaven and earth. Jesus is Lord, the same all-powerful, immutable Lord that was with Moses; "Pharaoh will not listen to you. Then I will lay my hand on Egypt and bring my hosts, my people, the children of Israel, out of the land of Egypt by great acts of judgment. The Egyptians shall know that I am the Lord when I stretch out my hand against Egypt and bring out the people of Israel from among them." (Exodus 7:4-5) The name is also used to refer to God, the Father, thus proving the deity of Jesus, as the Son, equal to the Father. Jesus is the Almighty "by creating all things but of nothing; by upholding all creatures in their beings; by the miracles he wrought on earth; by the resurrection of himself form the dead; by obtaining eternal redemption for his people." (Gill) Praise be to Jesus, the victorious Almighty. "Great and amazing are your deeds, O Lord

God the Almighty! Just and true are your ways, O King of the nations! Who will not fear, O Lord, and glorify your name? For you alone are holy. All nations will come and worship you, for your righteous acts have been revealed." (Revelation 15:3-4)

Prayer:

Lord Jesus, Almighty, You are the victorious commander of all the armies of heaven and earth. You are sovereign, omnipotent, immutable, and infinite. So great, are You Lord, and worthy of all praise and glory forever, amen.

The First and The Last

"When I saw him, I fell at his feet as though dead. But he laid his right hand on me, saying, "Fear not, I am the first and the last" Revelation 1:17

Jesus is reminding all who hear, He is the same Lord that spoke to the prophet Isaiah saying, "Thus says the Lord, the King of Israel and Redeemer, the Lord of hosts; 'I am the first and the last; besides me there is no god." (Isaiah 44:6) Jesus is everlasting; "the First by creation, the Last by retribution; the First because before Me there was no God formed; the Last because after Me there shall be no other; the First because from Me are all things; the Last because to Me all things return." (Richard of St. Victor) The Lord Jesus refers to Himself as the First and the Last three times in Revelation to express His eternity. It is a way for Him to say, "I always live – have lived through all the past, and will live through all whish is to come - and therefore I can accomplish all my promises, and execute all my purposes." (Barnes) In Jesus, the First and the Last, you have nothing to fear.

Prayer:

Lord Jesus, it is a comfort to know I have nothing to fear because You are the First and the Last; You are everlasting, there was none before You, and there will be no more to come; there is no God besides You. All Your promises are true, and You are faithful to complete them. All hope is found in You.

The Living One

"Fear not, I am the first and the last, and the living one. I died, and behold I am alive forevermore, and I have the keys of Death and Hades."
Revelation 1:17b-18

Jesus is not merely stating that He is alive but that He is the Living One, the One who conquered sin, death, and hell by His death and resurrection and is now "alive forevermore" holding "the keys of Death and Hades." All life, temporal and eternal, flow from Jesus, the Living One; "All things were made through him, and without him was not any thing made that was made, in him was life, and life was the light of men." (John 1:3-4) Jesus spoke many times about His power and authority as the Living One; "Jesus said to them, 'I am the Way, and the Truth, and the Life. No one comes to the Father except through me.'" (John 14:6) "Whoever believes in the Son has eternal life; whoever does not obey the Son shall not see life, but the wrath of God remains on him." (John 3:36) "Jesus said to her, 'I am the resurrection and the Life. Whoever believes in me, though he die, yet shall he live, and everyone who lives and believes in me shall never die." (John 11:25-26) As followers of Jesus, who believe and obey Him, we can be confident that we have eternal life with the Lord; we have nothing to fear. The tomb is empty; He is risen! Jesus holds "the keys of Death and Hades." He is alive; He is the Living One.

Prayer:

Praise Jesus, the Living One who conquered sin, death, and hell! I can rest in the knowledge that You hold the keys to Death and Hades; You have power and control over them. I have life because You are the Living One. Thank you, Lord Jesus, may all praise and honor and glory be Yours.

Him Who Holds the Seven Stars

"To the angel of the church in Ephesus write:
'The words of him who holds the seven stars
in his right hand, who walks among the seven
golden lampstands."
Revelation 2:1

Jesus had just explained, "As for the mystery of the seven stars that you saw in my right hand, and the seven golden lampstands, the seven stars are the angels of the seven churches, and the seven lampstands are the seven churches." (Revelation 1:20) Thus, the title declares He is the One who grasps their existence in His hand. Jesus is the One sending the messengers, the angels, to the churches to convey His love, support, and concern for them if they do not follow Him completely. "Christ knows and observes their state; though in heaven, yet He walks in the midst of his churches on earth, observing what is wrong in them, and what they want" (Henry) because He is the One who "holds the seven stars in his right hand, who walks among the seven golden lampstands."

Prayer:

Lord Jesus, Your love and concern for Your people and Your church is evident as You hold the stars and walk among the lampstands. You desire us to be with You, so You warn us to repent and follow You in complete obedience because You love us. Thank You for sending Your messengers; You are the One who holds the seven stars in His right hand.

Him Who has the Sharp Two-Edged Sword

> *"And to the angel of the church in Pergamum write: 'The words of him who has the sharp two-edged sword."*
> *Revelation 2:12*

Jesus is the One of whom "from his mouth came a two-edged sword." (Revelation 1:16) A two-edged sword cuts both ways, allowing it to penetrate and cut more deeply than any other ancient weapon. Jesus' Word, the Scripture, is the best and only weapon needed to fight the enemy's lies. "For the word of God is living and active, sharper than any two-edged sword, piercing to the division of soul and of spirit, of joints and of marrow, and discerning the thoughts and intentions of the heart." (Hebrews 4:12) Thus, Jesus gives us the same warning He gave the church of Pergamum, "Therefore repent. If not, I will come to you soon and war against them with the sword of my mouth." (Revelation 2:16) Jesus knows our deepest thoughts and intentions; we must stand on His Word and obey it completely.

Prayer:

Lord Jesus, Your Word is a sharp two-edged sword cutting to my heart, slicing away lies and falsehoods. So I repent and turn to You. You are my Savior. You are the Word; You are Truth; every word You speak is true. You are all I need to stand against the enemy.

True One

> "And to the angel of the church in Philadelphia write: 'The words of the holy one, the true one, who has the key of David, who opens and no one will shut, who shuts and no one opens.'"
> Revelation 3:7

The True One, translated from *alethinos* in Greek, means the "Very God as distinguished from the false gods and from all those who say they are what they are not." (Jamieson-Fausset-Brown Bible Commentary) Being True is one of the most important characteristics of our Lord and Savior, Jesus Christ; "And the Word became flesh and dwelt among us, and we have seen his glory, glory as of the only Son from the Father, full of grace and truth.(John bore witness about him, and cried out, "This was he of whom I said, 'He who comes after me ranks before me because he was before me.'")For from his fullness we have all received, grace upon grace. For the law was given through Moses; grace and truth came through Jesus Christ." (John 1:14-17) Jesus lavishes grace and truth upon us through eternal life, which He gives us by virtue of His death and resurrection. Jesus prayed, "Father, the hour has come; glorify your Son that the Son may glorify you, since you have given him authority over all flesh, to give eternal life to all whom you have given him. And this is eternal life, that they know you, the only true God, and Jesus Christ whom you have sent." (John 17:1-3) If Jesus is the True One, full of grace and truth, then all of His promises are true. We can have hope because He is the True One; "And we know that the Son of God has come and has given us understanding, so that we may know him who is true; and we are in him who is true, in His Son Jesus Christ. He is the true God and eternal life." (1 John 5:20)

Prayer:

Lord Jesus, You are the Holy One, the True One; all truth is found in You. You are the Very God, authentic and genuine. You cannot lie; You are faithful, trustworthy, and steadfast. I rest in the fact that all You say and do are true; all of Your promises are true. Everything You have done for me is true and will come to pass; I have eternal life because of You. You are True.

Who Has the Key of David

> *"And to the angel of the church in Philadel-*
> *phia write: 'The words of the holy one, the true*
> *one, who has the key of David, who opens and no*
> *one will shut, who shuts and no one opens.'"*
> *Revelation 3:7*

Hundreds of years before John received his prophetic vision, Isaiah was given one in which the Lord stated, "And I will place on his shoulder the key of the house of David. He shall open, and none shall shut, and he shall shut, and none shall open." (Isaiah 22:22) The angel Gabriel told Mary this would be her son, "And behold, you will conceive in your womb and bear a son, and you shall call his name Jesus. He will be great and will be called the Son of the Most High. And the Lord God will give to him the throne of his father David, and he will reign over the house of Jacob forever, and of his kingdom there will be no end." (Luke 1:31-33) Jesus is the One who holds the key; He is the True Master of the house of David; the Creator of the new Jerusalem, saying, "Behold, the dwelling place of God is with man. He will dwell with them, and they will be His people, and God Himself will be with them as their God." (Revelation 21:3) What He opens, no one or nothing can shut.

"Christ is faithful over God's house as a Son. And we are his house, if indeed we hold fast our confidence and our boasting in our hope." (Hebrews 3:6)

Prayer:

Lord Jesus, my confidence and hope are found in You because You hold the key of David; You are the Master of the house, and no one can overrule You; what You open, no one can shut, and what You shut, no one can open. You are in control; You are Sovereign. You are Lord; all honor and glory go to You.

Amen

*"And to the angel of the church in Laodicea
write: 'The words of the Amen, the faithful and
true witness, the beginning of God's creation.'"*
Revelation 3:14

Amen is used only here in Scripture as a personal name for Jesus, implying that He bears all the characteristics of the word; for "Amen means true, certain, faithful, and as used here, it means that he to whom it is applied is eminently true and faithful. What he affirms is true, what he promises or threatens is certain." (Barnes) "For all the promises of God find their Yes in him. That is why it is through him that we utter our Amen to God for his glory." (2 Corinthians 1:20) In Jesus, there is no guesswork or uncertainty; He affirms all that is faithful and true since the beginning. Jesus is the Amen.

Prayer:
Amen, all that is faithful and true, all the promises of God are affirmed in You, Lord Jesus. Therefore, certainty and truth are found in You, which is why we utter our Amen to the Amen for the glory of God.

Lion of Judah

"And one of the elders said to me, 'Weep no more; behold, the Lion of the tribe of Judah, the Root of David, has conquered, so that he can open the scroll and its seven seals.'"
Revelation 5:5

The Lion of the tribe of Judah is a reference that points all the way back to Jacob's (Israel's) blessing of his son, Judah; "Judah is a lion's cub; from the prey, my son, you have gone up. He stooped down; he crouched as a lion and as a lioness; who dares rouse him? The scepter shall not depart from Judah, nor the ruler's staff from between his feet, until tribute comes to him; and to him shall be the obedience of the peoples." (Genesis 49:9-10) The blessing speaks of a conqueror that will be descended from the tribe of Judah; Jesus is that descendent; His human lineage can be traced back to Judah. (See Matthew 1:1-17) Jesus holds the scepter as He sits on His throne, having conquered sin, death, and hell, where He states," I also conquered and sat down with my Father on His throne." (Revelation 3:21) The Lion of Judah is on His throne; He "has conquered, so that He can open the scroll and its seven seals;" therefore, we can "weep no more."

Prayer:

Lion of Judah, You have conquered sin, death, and hell; You hold the scepter, and to You shall be the obedience of the people. You are King; You alone are worthy to open the scroll. "Worthy are You, our Lord and God, to receive glory and honor and power." (Revelation 4:11) Amen

Root of David

"And one of the elders said to me, 'Weep no more; behold, the Lion of the tribe of Judah, the Root of David, has conquered, so that he can open the scroll and its seven seals.'"
Revelation 5:5

Jesus is the Root of David, "the root of Jesse, who shall stand as a signal for the peoples, of him shall the nations inquire, and his resting place shall be glorious. In that day the Lord will extend his hand yet a second time to recover the remnant that remains of his people." (Isaiah 11:10-11) Jesus is recovering the remnant as the signal the Lord "promised beforehand through his prophets in the Holy Scriptures concerning his Son, who was descended from David according to the flesh and was declared to be the Son of God in power according to the Spirit of holiness by his resurrection, Jesus Christ is our Lord, through whom we have received grace and apostleship to bring about the obedience of faith for the sake of his name among all the nations." (Romans 1:2-5) The Root of Davis has conquered and is worthy "to receive power and wealth and wisdom and might and honor and glory and blessing!" (Revelation 5:12)

Prayer:

Root of David, You are the promise fulfilled; You are re-covering the remnant of Your people through the mercy and grace shown on the cross and the gift of eternal life You gave through Your resurrection and defeat of death. May all that I do be for Your name to be heard among the nations and for You to receive power and wealth and wisdom and might and honor and glory and blessing! Amen.

King of the Nations

"And they sing the song of Moses, the servant of God, and the song of the Lamb, saying, 'Great and amazing are your deeds, O Lord God the Almighty! Just and true are your ways, O King of the nations!'"
Revelation 15:3

"Who would not fear you, O King of the nations? For this is your due; for among all the wise ones of the nations and in all their kingdoms, there is none like you...the Lord is the true God; he is the living God and the everlasting King." (Jeremiah 10:7,10) There is no one else like Jesus, the King of the nations; His deeds are great and amazing, His ways just and true; "for you were slain and by your blood you ransomed people for God from every tribe and language and people and nation and you have made them a kingdom of priests to our God." (Revelation 5:9-10) "For you alone are holy. All nations will come and worship you, for your righteous acts have been revealed." (Revelation 15:4) Therefore, Jesus, King of the Nations, can say, "from the rising of the sun to its setting, my name will be great among the nations...For I am a great King, says the Lord

of Hosts, and my name will be feared among the nations."
(Malachi 1:11,14)

Prayer:

Lord Jesus, King of the Nations, may we sing Your song,
the song of the Lamb, with those who have conquered. You
alone are holy; Your ways are just and true. All You are and all
You do is amazing; great are You, Lord; to You go all glory and
honor and praise.

Lord of lords and King of kings

> *"They will make war on the Lamb, and the Lamb will conquer them, for he is Lord of lords and King of kings, and those with him are called and chosen and faithful."*
> Revelation 17:14

Jesus is Lord of lord and King of kings by virtue of His nature as God. He is the sovereign ruler of all nations and tribes on earth; all the powers of heaven and hell are subject to His control. Some of those powers rebel and "make war on the Lamb," but "the Lamb will conquer" because "from his mouth comes a sharp sword with which to strike down the nations, and he will rule them with a rod of iron. He will tread the winepress of the fury of the wrath of God the Almighty. On his robe and on his thigh he has a name written, King of kings and Lord of lords." (Revelation 19:15-16) Jesus is "is the blessed and only Sovereign, the King of kings and Lord of lords." (1 Timothy 6:15)

Prayer:

Lord of lords and King of kings, to You go honor and eternal dominion. You alone are worthy. You are the conquering Lamb of God, from whose mouth comes a sharp sword with which to strike down those who make war against You. You are victorious; You have already won all the battles; Jesus, You are Lord of lords and King of kings!

Faithful and True

"Then I saw heaven opened, and behold, a white horse! The one sitting on it is called Faithful and True, and in righteousness he judges and makes war."
Revelation 19:11

All we understand of the meaning of the words "faithful" and "true" come from the person of Jesus Christ; they are not simply characteristics of Jesus; they are Jesus. "Faithful and True" is His name; He is the embodiment of the term. From the promise of victory made in the garden, "And I will put enmity between you and the women, and between your offspring and hers; he will crush your head, and you will strike his heel;" (Genesis 3:15) until Jesus rides out to declare His victory, once and for all, over Satan and his domains of sin, death, and hell, as described here in Revelation, the faithfulness of the Lord to redeem His people, is the overarching theme of the Bible. "For the word of the Lord is right and true, He is faithful in all He does." (Psalm 33:4) Jesus is the fulfillment of all the promises of the Lord. He is Faithful and True; "this name combines two characteristics: fidelity to promises, trustworthiness; and the power to satisfy every legitimate desire which has been awakened in the hearts of His people; for in Him all hopes find repose, and every ideal is realized." (Ellicott) So, we can have hope in the victory of the One who is Faithful and True because "the Lord is faithful, He will establish you and guard you against the evil one." (2 Thessalonians 3:3) Therefore, "let us hold fast to the confession of our hope without wavering, for He who promised is faithful." (Hebrews 10:23)

Prayer:

Lord Jesus, You are Faithful and True; everything I understand of what those words mean comes from You; they are You; everything else falls short in comparison. You are righteous in all that You do. You are the fulfillment of every promise from the Lord. I can hold fast to the hope found in You because You are Faithful and True.

Bright Morning Star

> "I, Jesus, have sent my angel to testify to you about these things for the churches. I am the root and the descendant of David, the bright morning star."
> Revelation 22:16

Jesus is the Bright Morning Star fulfilling the prophecy of Balaam; "I see him, but not now; I behold him, but not near: a star shall come out of Jacob and a scepter shall rise out of Israel;" (Numbers 24:17) and the promise given to Malachi; "But for you who fear my name, the sun of righteousness shall rise with healing in its wings." (Malachi 4:2) The Bright Morning Star from the line of Jacob has risen with healing in its wings, saying, "'Behold, the dwelling place of God is with man. He will dwell with them, and they will be his people, and God himself will be with them as their God. He will wipe away every tear from their eyes, and death shall be no more, neither shall there be mourning, nor crying, nor pain anymore, for the former things have passed away.' And he who was seated on the throne said, 'Behold, I am making all things new.' Also, he said, 'Write this down, for these words are trustworthy and true. No longer will there be anything accursed, but the throne of God and of the Lamb will be in it, and his servants will worship him. They will see his face, and his name will be on their foreheads. And night will be no more. They will need no light of lamp or sun, for the Lord God will be their light, and they will reign forever and ever.'" (Revelation 21:3-5, 22:3-5) Praise Jesus, the Bright Morning Star.

Prayer:

Bright Morning Star, thank You for bringing true healing by conquering sin and death; so that, You can fulfill the promise of no more pain or death. Thank You for wiping away every tear and for making all things new. My hope is found in You, Lord Jesus, Bright Morning Star; I long for the day that I will see Your face, and Your light will be all I need. Your words are trustworthy and true; You will reign forever and ever. Amen.

Final Blessing

I hope you have enjoyed learning some of the Amazing Appellations of Jesus and that your relationship with Him has grown more profound and more intimate. As I close this devotional, I wish to leave you with the prayer and blessing I have had for you during my time writing; it is taken from 1 John 5:31, Philippians 2:5-11, 2 Thessalonians 1:11-12, and Revelation 22:21.

> "I write these things to you who believe in the name of the Son of God, that you may know that you have eternal life. Christ Jesus, who, though He was in the form of God, did not count equality with God a thing to be grasped but emptied Himself by taking the form of a servant, being born in the likeness of man. And being found in human form, He humbled Himself by becoming obedient to the point of death, even death on a cross. Therefore, God has highly exalted Him and bestowed on Him the name that is above every name, so that at the name of Jesus, every knee should bow, in heaven and on earth and under the earth, and every tongue

confess that Jesus Christ is Lord, to the glory of God the Father. To this end, I always pray for you that God may make you worthy of His calling and may fulfill every resolve for good and every work of faith by His power so that the name of the Lord Jesus may be glorified in you and you in Him, according to the grace of God and the Lord Jesus Christ. The grace of the Lord Jesus be with all. Amen."

Bibliography

Barnes, Albert. "Barnes' Notes on the Whole Bible." 1870. *Bible Hub.* 22 November 2020.

Benson, Joseph. "Benson Commentary" 1857. *studylight.org.* 18 July 2021.

Calvin, John. "Calvin's Commentaries." n.d. *Bible Hub.* 15 October 2020.

Ellicott, Charles John. "Ellicott's Commentary for English Readers." 1905. *Studylight.org.* 18 June 2021.

Exell, Joseph S and Henry Donald Maurice. Spence-Jones. "The Pulpit Commentary." 1897. *StudyLight.org.* 28 November 2021.

Gill, John. 1999. *The New John Gill Exposition of the Entire Bible.* 28 October 2020.

Henry, Matthew. 1706. *Matthew Henry's Complete Commentary on the Whole Bible.* 8 November 2021.

"Jamieson-Fausset-Brown Bible Commentary." n.d. *BibleHub.org.* 1 November 2021.

MacLaren, Alexander. "Alexander MacLaren's Expositions of Holy Scripture." n.d. *studylight.org.* 3 September 2021.

Poole, Matthew. "Matthew Poole's Commentary of the Bible." n.d. *Bible Hub.* 12 December 2021.

Victor, Richard of St. Paris, n.d.

Kristina Howard-Booth has been a passionate Christ-follower for over thirty years. She began leading and speaking to groups while in high school, a trait that carried through college as an active member of the Baptist Campus Ministries at the University of Alabama. In 2003, the International Mission Board appointed Kristina and her husband to go to North Africa and the Middle East; since returning home, they have been a part of numerous short-term trips in the United States and abroad. Kristina's dedication to discipleship and encouragement has only grown over the last fifteen years; along with becoming a Certified Christian Life Coach, she has continued to lead youth and women's church groups. Kristina is currently pursuing her Masters of Biblical Theology through Southern Baptist Theological Seminary. She is a member of the Alabama Writers Cooperative and Hope*Writers. Kristina lives in Birmingham, Alabama, with her husband, daughter, and two dogs.

You can follow Kristina's work at @sojournersjourney20 on Instagram, FaceBook, and Pinterest or on her website at www.sojourner-sjourney.net.

CPSIA information can be obtained
at www.ICGtesting.com
Printed in the USA
JSHW031929190522
26003JS00001B/6